KT-130-534

Speaking of God

Trevor Dennis is now Canon Chancellor at
Chester Cathedral. He was Vice-Principal
and Tutor in Biblical Studies at Salisbury
and Wells Theological College between
1982 and the end of 1993. Before this he
studied at Cambridge and worked for seven
years as a school chaplain. He is married
with three daughters and a son. He writes
Bible reading notes for BRF's *Guidelines* and
his books include *Lo and Behold! The power
of Old Testament storytelling* (SPCK 1991)
and *Sarah Laughed: Women's Voices in the
Old Testament* (SPCK 1994).

WINCHESTER SCHOOL OF MISSION

06684

RESOURCE ROOM
CHURCH HOUSE
9 THE CLOSE
WINCHESTER
SO23 9LS
Tel: 01962 844644

Also by Trevor Dennis

Lo and Behold! The power of Old Testament storytelling
SPCK 1991
Sarah Laughed: Women's Voices in the Old Testament
SPCK 1994

Speaking of God
Trevor Dennis

First published 1992
Triangle
SPCK
Holy Trinity Church
Marylebone Road
London NW1 4DU

Second impression 1995

Copyright © Trevor Dennis, 1992

All rights reserved. No part of this book may
be reproduced or transmitted in any form or by
any means, electronic or mechanical, including
photocopying, recording, or by any information
storage and retrieval system, without permission
in writing from the publishers.

British Library Cataloguing in Publication Data
A catalogue record for this book is available from the British Library.
ISBN 0-281-04597-6

Typeset by Inforum Typesetting, Portsmouth
Printed and bound in Great Britain by
BPC Paperbacks Ltd
a member of
The British Printing Company Ltd

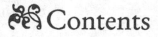 # Contents

❦ Introduction

Bright images of God, and the need for more

Just close your eyes and listen to this:

> . . . then the Lord God formed man of dust from the ground, and breathed into his nostrils the breath of life; and man became a living being (Genesis 2.7);

or this, from near the end of the very next chapter in Genesis:

> And the Lord God made for Adam and for his wife garments of skins, and clothed them (Genesis 3.21);

or this:

> And the Lord said [to Moses] 'Behold, there is a place by me where you shall stand upon the rock; and while my glory passes by I will put you in a cleft of the rock, and I will cover you with my hand until I have passed by; then I will take away my hand, and you shall see my back; but my face shall not be seen' (Exodus 33.21–23);

or take a look at the language of seduction and love-making used by God in the prophet Hosea's poems, as he looks forward to his eventual reconciliation with his people:

> 'Therefore, behold, I will allure her,
> and bring her into the wilderness,
> and speak tenderly to her' (Hosea 2.14);

or, most remarkably of all perhaps, this:

'For a long time I have held my peace,
    I have kept still and restrained myself;
now I will cry out like a woman in travail,
    I will gasp and pant.' (These words are put into
    God's mouth in Isaiah 42.14.)

We are not used to hearing of God compared to a woman in labour! We are not accustomed, or we think we are not accustomed, to images of God as vivid, as down to earth, as the ones in the quotations given here. And yet, whether we are Christians or Jews, these passages are in our scriptures, together with a vast number of other examples that are just as striking.

Alas, Christians have been given to understand that to speak of God in such obviously human terms is unsophisticated, naïve, silly, 'primitive'. The makers of Christian doctrine, back in the early centuries of the church, well versed in Greek and particularly Platonic philosophy, taught us to prefer abstract terms. The language of Christian doctrine became exceedingly complicated, of a kind only to be understood by the clever and the highly educated. Furthermore, still following the lead of Greek philosophy, the makers of doctrine saw their task as one of defining and refining, of drawing boundaries between what was right and what was wrong. They forgot, and they taught us to forget, that the writers of our scriptures, of both the Old and the New Testaments, were mostly poets or storytellers. They failed to recognise that the way the language of scripture works is the way poetry or storytelling works. Such language does not try to define. Instead, it seeks to evoke, to conjure up pictures in the minds of those who hear or read it. Its sophistication is the sophistication of high poetry, or of artful storytelling. It cannot be understood in a purely cerebral way, but it makes demands, sometimes very large demands, upon the imagination.

The biblical writers knew very well that God was not *literally* a pregnant woman, or a tailor, or a lover. They knew very well that he did not *literally* bend over the first man and give him the kiss of life, or hide his glory from Moses with the palm of his hand. They knew very well what they were doing. In writing in the way they did, they were not seeking to define God, or even describe him. They were dealing with metaphor, inventing images that had the mysterious power to evoke a sense of the God they had encountered. They were not attempting to pin God down, like a fading butterfly in a case. They were catching at his coat-tails, running after him with their bright words as he disappeared into his promised land and beyond. Their people had refused, remarkably for their day, to make a graven image of God, so they invented as many metaphors as they could, painting through their words a bewildering array of pictures, until in the Gospels of the New Testament they created the most extraordinary icon of all: the image of God as a man dying on a cross.

The longer I teach biblical studies, the more astonished I become by the artistry, the sophistication, the daring and the inventiveness of the biblical writers. Hosea, for example, who has already been quoted, pictures God as, among other things, a cuckolded husband, driven to distraction by his 'wife', Israel, as a farmer tending his vines, his figs or his palm trees, or looking after a favourite cow, as a parent bringing up a small child, or else as a lion roaring for his people's release from exile, or, more disconcertingly, as a leopard stalking his own people as his prey, or an enraged she-bear tearing them apart. At the very end of his little book, Hosea has God singing what is

3

quite clearly a love song to a male Israel, and so pictures 'him' as a woman in love.

If we are to be faithful to our scriptures, we must try to be as adventurous in our own talk of God as the biblical writers were. Too much of the language we come across in our liturgies, our hymns and our prayer books is predictable. The stock of images it uses is too small, its terms often drab, lifeless and, above all, too safe. If we are to make God seem exciting to those who believe, and intriguing to those on the edges of faith, then we must strive to be exciting and intriguing in our talk.

Yet it is not simply a matter of retelling the biblical stories and poems as vividly as we can. If we are faithful to our scriptures, we will not be content with the images we find there, however amazing their variety may be. The writers of the scriptures themselves were not content with what they inherited, but were always inventing new things, coining new metaphors, telling new stories, and working on new gospels; and ever since they finished, the Spirit of God has been incessantly calling us to new things, besides showing us the riches of the old.

Today many of us have become aware of a particular need for going beyond what the Bible provides. Of course, for Jews and Christians it will remain the most important and most universal source of inspiration. But it stems from a time when the dominance of men, at least in the public sphere, was taken for granted, and when people unquestioningly borrowed much of their talk about God from the corridors of power. God was inevitably 'king' and 'lord', when in fact (if we think about it and remind ourselves of his mystery) there is nothing inevitable about such language at all. There was and is both a sinister side and a tragic one to the huge preponderance of such power imagery. When Solomon built his temple in Jerusalem, he

4

built it as part of his palace complex. From then on God and king were joined together in holy (or was it unholy?) matrimony. From then on God was dressed in the trappings of a king, so that the king could behave like a god. Undoubtedly, in the history of the church, men in positions of authority have seen to it that the language of prayer and worship has been laden with words of power, partly to ensure the preservation of their own status and influence (and this in a church proclaiming a Son of God dying a criminal's death on a cross and only being given a decent burial because someone went out of his way to beg his body from the authorities!). The tragedy of the power talk is this: that in a world like ours, where there is so much suffering and disaster, and where at the same time so much more is under our control than it once was, God, the king, has come to seem either heartless and cruel, or else an irrelevance, pensioned off as a sad and lonely Lear, whose robes are faded and worn, and whose throne is full of woodworm.

But suppose, when we search for God, we start looking not for acts of power, but for acts of love. Suppose we come to God, not to fall on our knees, but to embrace and be embraced. Suppose we come to God as our Beloved and the world's Lover. If we start searching for God in love, will we not find just that: *a God in love*? And will we not find the deep longing, as large as the universe, that goes with that love, and will we not quickly discover the sharpness of God's pain, and will we not find the devastating power *in the love*? And will we not then find it perfectly natural, since we live in a world where women and men not only love, but love one another, to use images of God as a woman as well as a man? And, indeed, given the extraordinary power we find in images of God drawn from the human world, will we not seek avidly to

5

invent images from the female as well as the male side of that world? After all, despite the culture from which they come, our scriptures, particularly the Old Testament, give us a typically bold start with their talk of God as a woman in labour, or a woman singing a love song to her beloved (and those examples we quoted from Isaiah and Hosea are far from being the only ones we could have used).

Yet not only do we need to enrich our talk of God with more images drawn from the world of women, we also need to appeal more often to the non-human world. We are rediscovering our place on this planet. In certain quarters, we are becoming very uneasy about our human arrogance and sense of superiority over the rest of God's creation. Just as the predominance of male imagery for God has been used to preserve the status of men of power, so an exclusive or predominant use of human imagery is in danger of reinforcing our human pride and our notion that we have the right to behave like gods on God's earth. Again our scriptures help us to begin to look elsewhere. At the very start of Genesis, when the poet (he is best thought of as that) describes the spirit of God 'moving over the face of the waters' (Genesis 1.2), he uses a Hebrew word that makes us think of a bird flapping its wings, hovering over the surface. Another poet, the author of Psalm 91, pictures God as a bird, brooding its young: 'he will cover you with his pinions, and under his wings you will find refuge' (Psalm 91.4). I find such images compelling, and they, together with my experience of frequently tripping over God on bird-watching excursions, have led me to make fairly extensive use of their like in my own stories.

The history and the purpose of this book

My collection of stories contains only stories. Unlike the Bible, it has no poems. I hardly ever write poetry. In my

6

twenty years since ordination I have only twice written a sermon in blank verse. But over the past fifteen years I have preached a considerable number of sermons in the form of stories.

I started when I was a school chaplain in a boys' boarding school. Now teenage schoolboys are not renowned for their tact – at least not in the context of their weekday assemblies or Sunday worship. If they are listening, it is obvious. If they are not, there is no mistaking it. It is as if they have on/off switches in their jacket pockets, and the clicks can be well nigh audible. Many a time I had used a story *within* a sermon, as an illustration, or heard visiting preachers do the same. The technique is, of course, very common, but it had not worked well with these teenage boys. While the story was being told, so long as it had some colour to it, and was tolerably well told, the boys had listened. But when I reached the moral, the 'important' bit – the message the story was there to serve – the 'switches' had gone up, the eyes had glazed over, and the bottoms had starting fidgeting on the seats. I could see the problem, but no way round it, until one day a visiting preacher stood up, dived straight into a story, and *then sat down as soon as he had finished it*. 'That's how to do it!' I said to myself, and wished I was able to. For a long time I only *wished* I was able to, until for some reason (I dare not call it God's prompting: that would be to claim far too much) I decided to have a go. One result, after some considerable time, is this small book.

All the stories in this collection were written to be preached. Some date from my time as a school chaplain, although most of them emerged over the ten years when I was teaching Old Testament studies at Salisbury and Wells Theological College. For perhaps five of those ten years I contributed to the preaching

7

course at the college by discussing storytelling as a method of preaching, and by asking students to write 'story-sermons' of their own. Generally I gave little warning of the task, and they had to compose something overnight. At first I feared I was giving them an unreasonably tall order, especially since many of my own stories had rattled round in my head for some considerable time before finding their way on to the page and then to the chapel. My unease quickly evaporated, though, for the results were astonishing. Often one or two students in a group protested on the first day that writing stories was something they 'could not do', like maths or Japanese. Yet invariably they returned the next day having surprised themselves, and about to amaze the rest of us with a beautifully crafted piece.

In the summer of 1991 I went at least one step further in my demands. I had been asked to lead a day's conference on storytelling with a small group of lay people in Salisbury. When I was discussing the programme with Christine Farrington, the organiser of the conference, she encouraged me to leave forty-five minutes in the afternoon for the writing of stories. 'Forty-five minutes!' I exclaimed, 'but that's impossible!' But I knew her judgement was to be trusted, and somehow I managed to trust it. In the end we gave ourselves about fifty minutes. We all scribbled away, then went round the circle and read the results to one another. I remember one person had approached me when I had announced the task, to ask if she could work out a piece with someone else, since she would not be able to produce anything on her own. But when it came to it, I noticed her writing as busily as the rest of us. When her turn came to read it out, her story was enthralling, and we were all amazed by how colourful, how sharp, and often how profound everyone's contribution was.

I include this incident and recollections of my experiences in the college to make clear one major reason for my producing this collection: that is, to encourage others to have a go at composing stories for themselves and, if they are in the business of preaching, to consider using storytelling as one of their methods. There is an increasing interest in storytelling in the United States, and in some churches there its place in worship is being taken very seriously. In Britain, at least in the churches, it tends to be regarded as something for children, something for informal family services or for school assemblies. I hope this book is a reminder of what we all know already: that stories are just as powerful and important a means of communication for adults as for children.

I have, however, sometimes encountered a particular difficulty when preaching these stories to adult congregations. Some people expect to find a moral in each of them, and are confused and somewhat frustrated when they cannot spot one. It is not particularly surprising that this should be so. After all, many people expect sermons of any kind to make points. Furthermore, many Christians have been taught that Christ's parables are stories with a moral, though they are far too subtle and alive to be just that. Yet further, Sunday by Sunday they are treated in the lessons to fragments of scripture that have been specially cut out of their contexts to make particular points, and often they read in their pew sheets what those points are supposed to be. In fact, most of the biblical material is not didactic, and is not there to make points at all, but to create strange new worlds and invite us to step across their thresholds. Those worlds are inhabited by God, and they, the storytellers and poets, hoped that having entered them we might catch something of his mystery, and encounter something of the truth about ourselves and the strange-but-familiar world in which we ourselves live. If it does not seem too pretentious to say it, the stories in this little book have been written with a similar purpose, and the same hope. They seek to pay tribute to the inventiveness and creativity of the biblical writers, since they draw their chief inspiration from their stories and images, and spend most of their time reworking them, mixing them, or overlaying them with images from modern painting or poetry, or from the author's own experience.

If they help readers to look at the Bible with fresh eyes, then the stories will have done some of their work. If, through divine grace, they make God sharp, exciting and real, or rather, remind us how sharp and exciting and real God has always been and always will be, then they will have done a bit more of it. If they also enable people to discover their own powers of storytelling, and stimulate them to do much better themselves, then they will have done enough.

❦1 The Garden of God

> In the beginning God created the heavens and the earth.
> The earth was without form and void, and darkness was
> upon the face of the deep; and the Spirit of God was
> moving over the face of the waters. (Genesis 1.1–2)

The first bit is clear enough perhaps, but what of the
second? Does the Hebrew speak of the Spirit of God
hovering over the waters of chaos, or does it speak of
those waters being shaken by the wind of God? Well, the
truth is that it speaks of both. It contains genuine am-
biguity. But to my ear the words whisper of yet something more. I suspect there is another meaning lurking
here.

What if the chaos was shaken into order by the gale of
God's laughter? What if the fish and the whales were
made to swim in the depths of that laughter, and the birds
to float on its upcurrents and tumble in its eddies as jackdaws do about a cathedral spire? Why, then, human
beings, made in God's image, modelled upon him, came
from the heart of his laughter. Why, then, we were made
to bring a smile to the face of the earth, to bring the
blessing of laughter wherever we go.

If this was so, if this *is* so, then how might the rest of the
story go? Might it go something like this?

*   *   *

For a time, for a moment, for the twinkling of an eye in
God's garden, in Eden, laughter prevailed. When man and
woman first saw one another, they laughed, and her first
words to him were these:

'Arise, my love, my fair one,
    and come away;
for lo, the winter is past,
    the rain is over and gone.
The flowers appear on the earth,
    the time of singing has come,
and the voice of the kookaburra
    is heard in our land.'[1]

But too soon, too soon, the sound of laughter became, through disobedience, the scurrying of bewilderment and fear, and turned into the din of accusation, and then into the cacophony of curse, pain, toil, subordination and expulsion. The garden became empty, its kookaburras called no more, and all that could be heard in the cool of the day was the sound of God's weeping.

After Eden, violence grew like a weed upon the earth, until it covered its whole surface. Laughter was strangled on earth and in heaven also, and the whole creation was drowned in the flood of God's tears.

A few survived, a handful, and God thought he would teach them to laugh again by showing them how to plant a vineyard and grow grapes and make wine. But the wine of that laughter also turned sour at its first tasting,[2] and God was compelled to begin again. So he took a man called Abraham and his barren wife Sarah, and he said to them, 'Get on your camels and go, and when you, Abraham, are a hundred, and you, Sarah, ninety, I will bring smiles to your faces, and you will bring laughter into my world.'

They did not believe him, of course. Abraham laughed in his face – not with the glee of the newly created man and woman in the garden, but with derision and mockery.[3]

Yet the glint in God's eye remained, and Sarah conceived and bore a son, Isaac, whose name means 'he

12

laughs'. And Sarah said, 'God has made laughter for me; everyone who hears will laugh over me.' (Genesis 21.6)

She knew the ribald remarks that would be made. Nudge, nudge, wink, wink, 'Have you heard, old Sarah's had a baby!' 'No! Who's the father?' 'Abraham.' 'Abraham! Stone me, what's he been taking?' And so on. The laughter God made for Sarah was not for the pious, not for the clever, not for the polite, but for the old crones round the well, a ribald, rib-tickling, thigh-slapping laughter, enough to catapult the dentures on to the sand.

But the laughter God made for Sarah was shaped also to put an end to the disgrace of her barrenness (for that is how it was regarded then), to give her a status and a sheer joy that for years she had given up for lost. With Isaac, Sarah found herself back in Eden, back in God's garden, noisy once more with the laughing cries of the kookaburras.

Yet Sarah had spoken only part of the truth. Through Isaac's birth God had made laughter not only for her, but for the world. And though for a spell Sarah found herself back in Eden, the world did not. A new era did not dawn with Isaac's birth, except in the matter of God's disappointment and bewilderment. He had to try yet again. Yet another ploy.

So he summoned Moses to the top of Sinai, and there he told him all his jokes and all his funny stories. And Moses came to the foot of the mountain with tears rolling down his cheeks, and opened his mouth and said, 'Thus says the Lord, "Did you hear the one about the . . .?" ' but he got no further. The people had made a god for themselves that told no jokes, had no funny stories, a god that had become the centre of stern-faced, pompous ritual, where there was no laughter, only hysteria.[4]

So God returned to weep in his garden in the cool of the day, and, rocking himself in his misery, he sang:

13

'. . . my soul is full of troubles,
   and my life draws near to Sheol.
I am reckoned among those who go down to the
   Pit. . . .
Thou, O Man, hast put me in the depths of the Pit,
   in the regions dark and deep.
Thy wrath, O Woman, lies heavy upon me,
   and thou dost overwhelm me with all thy waves.'[5]

The kookaburras heard and fell silent.

There was nothing for it but for God to take flesh and come among us.

He came to teach his world to laugh. Those who shared his misery caught his glee. It drew them out from among the tombs,[6] out from their hiding places in the hills. To keep company with that laughter was for them like being able to see again, to hear and to speak, to run and to dance, when once they had been blind, deaf, dumb, lame or paralysed. With that laughter they found themselves in Eden, no longer afraid, no longer despairing. They were lords in God's garden, fine ladies walking his terraces. They had never known, never heard, anything like it in all their born days.

But there were others who wished once and for all to wipe the smile off God's face, and put a stop to his nonsense. So they made a fool out of him . . .

. . . But it is the job of the fool, the jester, to make others laugh. That is and was the irony of it. And that was why early one morning some women found God's tomb in the garden bursting with his merriment.

2 The Flock

The houses of the town keep their backs to the sea, and its people fasten their eyes on their work, or stare at nothing. But someone occasionally takes the track across the marsh that leads to the sea wall. There they find her, with her hair shining in the bright winter's sun, and her shadow stretching long over the water. She knows nothing of the puffing pride of the town, but spans with her fingers the vastness of the sky and runs her hand over the deep swell of the sea. She catches the glint in the bird's eye, and keeps pace with the darting fish. She can smell faintly the earth's decay, yet she can also crack it open to reveal the white, firm freshness within. She is the child in us, the child that gets lost in the dark streets of the town, but can be found always on the long sea wall.

I found her that winter's day with her hair dancing in the bright wind and her shadow floating gently on the water. The tide was in. The rains had washed the sky clean and scrubbed the sea blue, and the long sun lent gold to the gulls' backs. A few ducks were preening themselves on the edge of a pool to the landward side of the wall. A curlew called. It was the birthday of the earth.

I turned my back on the water to watch the ducks combing their feathers. She, however, stood looking along the wall to the west. She saw them coming when they could hardly be seen at all. I with my eyes on the ducks saw nothing until a loud rushing of wings made me turn round. A few yards out from the wall a flock of birds hurtled past us, flying low over the water.

With my adult mind I recognised them as dunlin, small wading birds, and knew they could keep up this mad-cap flight till the tide receded and the mud returned with its rich food for their probing bills. I reckoned the flock must number two or three hundred birds. I had seen dunlin many times before, and soon I would turn back to the ducks. But the child touched my elbow and told me to keep watching.

The flock turned suddenly away from the wall across the open sea, and turned and turned again. The birds were grey brown above and white beneath, but in that winter sun they shone gold and silver. Each time they banked they turned from one to the other, from silver to gold, from gold to bright silver. They moved always as one, yet they seemed to follow no one bird's lead. As one turned, so all turned, from silver to gold, from gold to silver. Far to the east they flew, till they ceased to be a flock of birds at all, but became instead a gold, now silver, cloud, folding, ever refolding itself into new and exquisite forms. Farther to the east they flew. Now when they showed the upper part of their wings, the gold was lost in the light of the sun shining off the sea. But when again they banked, the silver of their bodies and their underwings danced like small stars. One after another, new constellations were made, until even the silver was too far off for my eyes, and only the sea and the sky were left.

Yet still the child watched the flock go, and stood waiting for its return. 'There are not many days,' she said, 'when he passes so close. But then, this is the earth's birthday.' She strained her eyes after the birds.

'When Moses asked to see his glory,' she continued, 'he put him in a cleft of the rock and shielded his eyes with his hand.[7] There is nowhere here for us to be hidden, and nothing to shade our eyes. Yet he passed us by, a few

16

yards from where we stand. This is indeed the birthday of the earth.'

'Then which of the birds was he?' I asked. 'I could see no leader. They moved as one, but I saw none show them which way to turn.'

'Then stop trying to identify him,' the strange child replied. 'He was, he is, the flock itself. He was and is its light, now gold, now silver in the winter sun, now stars dancing over the water, now only a waiting. He hides himself in the flock. You cannot pick him out. If you try, you deny the divinity of the rest. Do not try to identify him. Do not try to capture him, and hold him prisoner in your clever mind. You can never tell him from the others. He is the flock, and he hides himself in the flock. He is most elusive, and he is there plain for you to see. He is most insignificant, yet he makes all divine. You never know which one he is. So you must treat each one as if it's him. That's all. Then you will find him.' She paused, then grasped my hand and cried, 'Look, the flock is coming back!' She led my eyes to where the stars were beginning to dance again.

The track I took that day leads back to the dark streets, and to the people bent over their work, seeing nothing. But it will take those who wish to the sea wall, to the child with her hair shining in the bright winter's sun, to the flock turning and flickering over the water, and to the one who hides so shyly, so very beautifully, the glory of his divinity.

❧3 Divine Images

They got back to the village just as dawn broke. No one saw them arrive, not even the birds, but the news very soon got around. 'They're back!' was passed from house to house, and the cat said, 'Come on! Let's get them all together and find out what they have seen.'

There was a flying and a scampering of feet in all directions, and soon the entire village was gathered on the green, the villagers grouped in a circle with the travellers in the middle.

'Did you see him?'

'Yes.'

'What was he like?'

'Bet you didn't get very far, Sluggy!' said the dog, and the others laughed. 'Unless the fox gave you a ride!' and they laughed even harder.

'It wasn't that kind of journey,' the fox said. 'It was as hard for me as it was for Sluggy, and speed made no difference. I ran, and he slid, and we got there together.'

The crowd did not understand that. The dog asked again, 'What was he like?'

'Black!' said the slug. 'You have never seen such a black! Glistening it was, in its own light!'

'What do you mean, "in its own light"? Was he a glow-slug?' They laughed again.

'No . . . well, kind of, though he had more than just a glow. A shining, that's what he had, a shining, so that we didn't need the sun. His was all the light we needed. A black sun! Just imagine! A black sun! But that's what he was, resplendent' (the slug had a sudden attack of poetry) 'in his sluggishness!' They roared with laughter.

'I think you mean "slugness",' said the cat.

'Do I? "Resplendent in his slugness". All right. Doesn't sound as good as "sluggishness", though.'

'We know what you mean, Sluggy,' said the fox. 'Where you found slugness, I found foxness. Sheer, unadulterated foxness, except . . .' He paused. 'His angels were . . .' He stopped.

'Were what, Fox?' asked the mole, and then he added softly, 'Chickens?'

The crowd fell over itself in laughter, but the fox smiled at the mole and said, 'You're a wise old mole. I might have guessed you'd get it right.'

'Do you mean to tell us they *were* chickens?' said the dog. 'Now I've heard everything!'

'No you haven't. No you haven't,' came the still, small voice of the butterfly. 'You haven't heard the half of it. You will never hear the half of it. But listen to what I and Snake and Eagle and Man have to say.

'When I first saw him I almost missed him, he was so far from what I expected. He was just . . . No, that is wrong. There is no "just" with him, only "is", only "am".'

'Leave out the philosophy, Butterfly!' cried the goat. 'What was he just, or not just?'

'A chrysalis,' replied the butterfly. 'I didn't know what it was at first, but then it stirred, or something stirred inside it, and a fragment of memory was shaken free within me, so that I knew what I would see next. And yet, as it turned out, I did not know.'

'He's going philosophical again!'

'No. Give him a chance. Go on, Butterfly.' It was the mole's voice again.

19

'I did not know, I did not expect, such a butterfly as he was. His wings grew large, and as he spread them out I saw on each a great eye which caught me and held me in its gaze. The colour of those wings, of those eyes! Oh, the colour of them! And this is strange. You would have thought I would have felt my drabness beside his beauty, but no. He showed me not my drabness, but my own beauty, and I saw that it was a reflection of his.'

'It was like that for me,' added the snake, 'or nearly so. For me he was, as you might have guessed, a snake, but one who was continually sloughing his skin. Each skin was more beautiful than the last, until I felt I could take in no more, and shut my eyes. Even in my darkness the colours flashed and shone, then suddenly all went dark, and I opened my eyes. Do you know how I saw him then? A worm! What I would before have called "just a worm", a "common-or-garden-just-a-worm", a "dull, boring worm". But I learned then what Butterfly has learned, that there is no "just" with him.' A worm hiding at the back of the crowd suddenly felt rather pleased with herself.

'She taught me that, too.' It was the eagle's turn now. 'When first I found her, she was an eagle of towering majesty. High, high up she was, much higher than I have ever been. Then, as she descended, her great wings came to enfold us, embracing not just us, but the whole world. All was held in those wings of hers, and none had any fear of beak or talon. Yet the touch of her feathers made me tremble. Like Snake, I closed my eyes. Can you guess what made me open them again? A tickling on my beak! There she was, a bluetit hanging upside down on my great beak! I could have given a quick flick and swallowed her down in one! Well, no. But that's what you might have thought. To have God doing acrobatics on your beak!

Just imagine, just imagine! It does something for you, I can tell you.'

During all this the man had not said a word. He was the only one of the travellers who seemed tired by the journey. He sat there with his head resting on his hands, enveloped in his own sad bewilderment.

The fox nudged him. 'They want you to speak now. They're waiting for you. The rest of us have had our say.'

The man looked up at the silent faces round him. 'They understand what they have seen,' he said quietly. 'Slug, Fox, Butterfly, Snake, Eagle – they all understand. I do not yet understand. That is why I sit here with my head in my hands, for I want to understand as they do. I sense that when I do, I will find what they have found, and their joy will be mine also.'

'But what did you see?' asked the mole. 'Was it not a man?'

'Yes, it was a man.'

'Well then?'

'But he was hanging on a cross. We had crucified him.'

❧ 4 Lord of the Dance

And God said, 'Let there be . . .' And there *was*, and he fell over himself in his joy. His hand flashed, and a kingfisher flew. It flashed again, and another kingfisher flew, more brightly coloured still, again and another kingfisher, and again and another. There was no end to them! What strange exuberance! What extravagance! What prodigality! What sheer delight!

He hurled the stars into their spaces, and he knelt down to form between finger and thumb intricate, shining beetles. He danced in the river air with the mayflies and rode the great oceans on the backs of the whales. He slid deep down into the very dark with strange, luminous creatures that to him were not strange at all. They too came from the bright world of his imaginings. He swung from the trees with the orang-utans and rested on the seventh day with the sloths. He banistered down the swirl of a galaxy one moment and played hermit crab the next, hiding himself away with the smallest of the creatures left by the tide in the rock pools.

Wherever he went on the land he left his footprints, mounds of thyme and banks of cowslip, harebell and rock-rose. He spent a year of his eternity making grasses. And still his imagination was not exhausted, and still his fingers worked, and still he fell over himself with delight. What absurd exuberance! What extravagance! What prodigality! What sheer, sheer joy!

He was spending one sabbath day with the sloths as usual, when a new thought came to him. This would be his sabbath child. He watched the chimpanzees playing on the floor of the forest beneath him. He pictured to himself what they would be like clean-shaven. In his mind's eye he took a razor to them. Yes, this would be his sabbath child.

He dropped down to the ground, then went out of the forest into the middle of a field and sat down. Among the flowers and the grasses he took forefinger and thumb and began to work.

He always made two of everything. So he made two of them, and hugged them and told them that when they had been fruitful and multiplied a bit he would introduce them to the delights of the eightsome reel. He had been longing for an eightsome reel, but really the kangaroos were hopeless and the rabbits quite ridiculous at it. The eagles and the kites could do it in the sky, but far too slowly for his liking. 'Come back here in a few years' time with your children,' he said, 'and we will do an eightsome reel together, and the stars will sing, I promise you, and the nightingales will be their usual selves, and the rabbits will be even more ridiculous than they are already!'

But a few years later they did not appear. He waited, but they did not come. In the end he went into the forest to look for them. He called and called, but there was no reply.

Eventually he returned to the edge of the forest, and it was then that he saw them, running across the field away from him. 'Where are you going?' he cried, but they only ran faster. 'Where are you going?' and they ran and ran. But, of course, you cannot outrun God. He caught them up as they were crossing the dancing floor he had prepared. A third time he asked them, 'Where are you going?'

Their lips scarcely moved in reply. 'We were afraid,'[8] they said.

23

For the first time in all creation those brief words stopped God in his tracks. The human family turned to escape, and he was left alone in the middle of the dancing floor.

Next day, when the sun came up, the whole field was red with poppies.

✤5 God's Expulsion

They sat on the bank, making patterns on the surface of the water with their toes. A thrush sang from the top of the tree the far side of the river, deepening the silence with its song. The rushes bent lightly to the stream, the moorhen chicken-necked its way across, and the kingfisher flew and warmed itself in the sun. The river lay back in its bed, hiding its turbulence, and they felt, the two of them, that they could sit there for ever.

'Is this the Pishon, or the Gihon, dear?' he asked, 'or the Euphrates, or the Tigris?'[9]

'I don't know,' she said. 'God did the naming of the rivers, and we haven't got a map.'

'Pity. I like to know where I stand.'

'Sit, dear.'

'Pardon?'

'Never mind.' She paused, and flicked a splash of water with her foot. 'You didn't make a very good job of naming the animals, did you, dear. Fancy calling the cheetah a "long-tailed sloth"!'

'It was lying down at the time.'

'And the hippopotamus was most upset when you called it a "dodo".'

The man stood up. 'Come on,' he said. 'We've got work to do.'

'And what made you think the hedgehog was a "black-tailed godwit"?'

'It had a black tail.'

'It didn't. The cat was lying behind it.'

'Oh.'

'Anyway, the black-tailed godwit's a bird.'

'Oh.'

'So's the dodo, come to that.'

'Yes, all right, I'm sure it is! I told him he should have put you on naming the animals. You're much better at it than me.'

'But I wasn't there at the time, remember? You had a full set of ribs then.'

They walked in silence for a while, till they came to the tree in the middle of the garden. Its shade was too enticing, as always it was, and they put down their hoes and lay down beside the trunk and gazed up at the sky through the tangle of branches and leaves.

'Will it always be like this?' he asked.

'What do you mean?'

'Like this,' and he waved his hand in a lazy circle above his head.

'I don't expect so.'

'Why not?'

'Because you'll want this place to yourself one day.'

'No I won't. I'll want you here. And our children, when we have them,' and he touched her lightly on the thigh.

'But you won't want *him* here.'

'Why not?'

'Because he planted it, and you want it to be of your own making.'

'No I don't. I'm perfectly happy just keeping it in good order, the way he wants it.'

'Exactly.'

'Exactly what?'

'The way *he* wants it.'

'But that's the way I want it, too.'

'You *did*, but you've changed. There's a new look in your eye. You've already decided this is *your* place – or will be some day.'

The leaves of the tree stirred uneasily above them and a flock of doves in its crown woke suddenly and clattered off. The woman's words came to a stop in the man's brain: 'You've already decided this is *your* place – or will be some day.' The words had entered his head some time before. They had already given rise to the look in his eye that she had seen. He had not thought she noticed such things; he must have underestimated her. Now the words stopped wandering about aimlessly in his head, and set up home there.

So it was that while the woman worked in the Japanese garden building a tea-house, he built a fence. And when she moved to the rockery and channelled the Euphrates through it in a delightful series of waterfalls, he still built a fence. And while she planted a vineyard and trained the kangaroos to jump up and down on the grapes in the vat, he still built his fence. And when she had just made a large and intricate maze in the middle of a wood, so that she and the man and God could play at hide-and-seek and fill the trees with their laughter, he finished the fence and nailed his notices on it. 'No Trespassers!' they read. He looked at them and smiled. The fence went right round the garden. Now it was his. He went in search of the woman.

It was not hard to find her. Yells of glee were coming from the maze, and a hundred jackdaws were tumbling in delight above it as the woman and her God chased one another round the hedges. Now another look came into the man's eye. The woman had seen hints of his ambition, but she had not caught sight of his jealousy. His eyes were now dark with it, and his voice harsh with its tones.

'Come out of there, you two!' he shouted. 'Get out! Get out!'

The woman and her God eventually emerged hand in

hand, and looked the man in the eye.

The man paused. 'Get out,' he said quietly. 'Get out. The gate's over there. The snake will open it for you.'

They did not move. His voice fell to a whisper. 'Get out.'

God and the woman walked slowly in the direction in which the man was pointing. As they neared the gate, the woman slipped her hand out of his.

'I must stay here,' she said.

God hesitated, glanced at her face, and passed through the gate on his own.

The man, suddenly trembling, went to lie down in the shade of the tree in the middle of the garden. The ground was thick with its leaves. It was dead.

The woman sat on the bank, making patterns on the surface of the water with her toes.

❦6 After Eden

The heat of the afternoon was lifting. The air was beginning to stretch and stir itself into action. Soon it would be the best part of the day.

The snake was the first to sense him coming. Beneath his coils the earth gave a tremor which he recognised at once. It was God's footstep. He had cast off many a skin since he had last felt it, but how could he forget it? It was unmistakable. He flicked his tail and hissed gently. The old woman opened an eye, and closed it again. She was getting deaf. The snake hissed more loudly.

'What's the matter with you?' she said, 'It's not time yet.' Her siestas had been getting longer.

'It's him,' the snake whispered. 'It's *him*, and he's coming this way.'

No response.

The snake raised his head and rubbed himself gently against her heels.

'That tickles!' she cried. 'Now look what you've done! You've gone and woken me up, and it's another hour till teatime! There's no chance I'll get back to sleep now.' Slowly she swung her feet down and stood up. Then she felt the trembling of the ground and heard the footsteps. 'Heavens above! Why didn't you tell me? Adam! Adam! Wake up, you old fool! God's coming and I haven't even got my dentures in! Adam!' She poked him with her stick. Adam groaned. She poked a bit harder. Adam only groaned louder. She poked him so hard he fell off his chair.

'What the . . .?'

'Listen!'

Adam listened. He tapped his hearing aid and listened again. Still nothing. He stamped his feet to get the circulation going. Then he felt it, too. That movement in the earth.

'God Almighty!'

'Exactly! Go and put the kettle on, while I find my teeth! And there are some cakes in the tin. Put them on a plate. And use a doily! Oh, dear! If I'd known he was coming, I'd have baked something special, or you could have made some of your biscuits.' She scurried off in the direction of the bathroom.

Adam did not know what to do, but went to the kitchen to do it anyway. The snake slid after him. Now where was the cake tin? She was always putting it in funny places. Which tea would he prefer, he wondered? Chinese or Indian? Well, they only had the usual teabags, so that would have to do. He peered out of the kitchen window. He was not coming from that direction – but then he wouldn't come from there, would he? He didn't go to Eden any more. Not since they'd turned it into a theme park. He sighed and poured the milk into a jug.

'Get a move on, dear! I don't know, the snake could do it faster than you! Is my hair all right? I changed my dress, and put some shoes on. Here, give it to me! What? I've forgotten my teeth? Oh! I've forgotten my teeth!'

'I'll get them for you,' said Adam. 'You finish getting the tea.' The old snake smiled indulgently. The earth stirred uneasily beneath them.

A short time later they were at the door, ready at last to greet him. Adam straightened his tie.

'Have you noticed you're not afraid of him any more?' said the snake.

'We're too old for that,' Adam replied.

'Just want to do things properly, that's all,' replied Eve. 'And *you* haven't slid behind the sideboard, either,' she said to the snake.

They waited. Adam took Eve's hand.

They had taken a long time to forgive him. He had blamed her, she had blamed the snake, the snake had failed to find anyone to blame, but once out of Eden all three of them had blamed God. Everything had been against them then, especially him. It had been a long time before they had seen what they had done. Then they had found it hard to live, harder to live with themselves. They had forgiven God and forgiven each other, but it had been well-nigh impossible to forgive themselves. In the end, in their old age, they had succeeded, but the strange loneliness had not gone away. In the evenings the lights of Eden were clearly visible above the horizon, and when the wind was in the right direction they could even hear the sounds of the fun fair. Yet that only made things worse.

They had not seen him since that day. 'Why's he coming now? What does he want of us?' At least they were not afraid of him now. 'Hope the cakes are all right. They're not terribly fresh.'

The snake hissed quietly.

'What's the matter?'

'There's something wrong. It's him all right, but his step doesn't sound like it did. He's limping.'

The old woman and her husband peered into the distance, and all of a sudden a new fear gripped them. They were not afraid for themselves this time. They were afraid for him.

They were looking in the wrong direction. He was approaching from behind the house, but the sound of his steps echoed back from the low hills. They did not see him till he came round the corner of the house, and almost collapsed at their feet.

'Dear God!' cried Adam and Eve and the snake. 'What have they done to you?'

❧7 The Lost Son[10]

They stood at the water's edge, gazing over the sea, looking at nothing. The sun was getting high, and the mist, which in a few hours would blot out the mountains on the far side, was itself beginning to rise. Behind them, on the very top of the ridge, three vultures waited for the thermals and kept sharp eyes open for signs of new death. No fish broke the surface of the water.

'This place has been dead for years, for millennia,' she said. 'You can tell. There are no kingfishers. Everywhere you look in Galilee there are kingfishers. The whole world down here is dead.'

'All the towns round here are in ruins,' said the man. 'Burned to a cinder. Do you think one of them was the city he built, the place he named after his son?'[11]

She did not know. Perhaps. It was always 'perhaps'. They never got any further than 'perhaps'.

'Where shall we go next?' he asked, speaking more to himself than to her.

They looked out over the water. There was no life to be seen anywhere.

'We had no chance to say "goodbye",' she said. She had said it a thousand times, and each time it was true. 'Two sons in one day. Two grown sons. We heard the earth crying, didn't we? That was when we knew something was wrong. By the time we found the body, he had gone.

'It had seemed so good, so unexpected. We had wondered whether it would work outside the garden, but it did, didn't it, and we had those two fine boys, so quickly.

We hardly had to wait at all. First one, then the other. And they grew up good and strong. They began to go their separate ways, of course, but we were still a family together – until that day when the earth started crying. It wouldn't stop. Just went on and on. It came to a flood in the end.'

'And that didn't change things.' He had heard it all before, but he wanted to hear it again.

'His own brother! How could he kill his own brother, and dig him into the ground like that? No wonder he couldn't show his face afterwards. But we didn't know he was going off for good. Two sons in one day. No explanation, no farewells, no forwarding address. Just reports much later that he had married and had a son, and had built a city and named it after the boy. If we knew the boy's name, we might have a chance of finding the place, and surely the people would know where he lived.' She sat down on a rock. 'No kingfishers,' and she shook her head.

To the north of the sea was a large oasis, and from there a road led up into the desert hills. It was notorious for its thieves who lay in waiting for travellers, but the couple's grief enveloped them and protected them from any thought of their own safety. Up in the hills the air was cooler. A shepherd piped his flock down towards a stream in the bottom of a dark valley.

They reached the city at the other side of the desert just before the ninth hour. It was strangely dark for the time of day. They remarked upon it, and then were suddenly afraid. Once again they heard that same ancient crying of the earth. The road had led them from death to death. Once again, after an hour's searching, they found the body, this time at the top of a low hill outside the city walls. There had been no hurried burial. The man still hung where they had hung him. He was not the only one. There were two more of them, one already dead, like him. Small groups of women huddled at the feet of their two crosses.

Stumbling in the shadows, the woman and the man went across to the third figure. He was alone, some way apart. For him there were no women to watch him die.

Even in the dark they recognised him at once. They had found him – after all that time. They had so nearly given him up for lost. They wanted to hold him, as they had used to do when he was small and had hurt himself, but his feet were all they could reach to embrace. Yet that was enough. He knew them, and for the first time that day he started to weep. 'I must tell you,' he said. 'I won't have to escape any more. I can stay there. I will belong there. He said so.' The words were costing him all the strength he had left. 'He has shown me how to be my brother's keeper, you see. Better late than never. He says I will be with him today in Eden. I always wanted to know what it was like. After all you told me about it.' They hardly caught his last words. His head suddenly fell to one side.

Beneath the feet of the man and the woman the ground stopped its crying.

❦ 8 The Storm

'Can you take me to the edge of the world?' I said.

They laughed and went back to their beer.

'Can you take me to the edge of the world?' I repeated.

They looked at me strangely, and gave me directions to the local psychiatric hospital.

'Can you take me to the edge of the world?'

She searched through the looks in my eyes. 'Do you really wish to go there?'

'Yes.'

'It is a fearful place.'

'I wish to go there.'

'It is a most fearful place.'

'I wish only to look and to listen. I wish only to have gone there, to the very edge of the world, to have seen and to have heard for myself.'

'Very well. But it will not be as you expect.'

She led the way, beyond the town, beyond the fields, beyond the forest, beyond the bare moorland beyond, and we began to climb a ridge of hard, black rock.

Suddenly she stopped. 'I will leave you now,' she said. 'Unless you want to return with me, for it is a most fearful place.'

'No. I will go on.'

'Then may God bless you.'

With that she turned and went back the way we had come. I watched her go until she was very small, and then I faced the ridge once more.

The climb was difficult. The sky darkened as I went higher, and a roar began to fill my ears. At last, exhausted,

I crawled on to the top of the ridge, and stopped, gripping the rock in terror.

I was on the lip of a precipice, that fell in one fall into the abyss of an ocean in fury. Raising my eyes, I could see no horizon. The world was filled with this sea, with its roar and dreadful crash.

I knew where I was, yet these were not the waters of chaos from which God had called forth the world.[12] This was the ocean of his anger, beating itself against the sharp, ugly rock of our brutality, hurling itself against our blindness and ignorance, against the tall cliffs of our arrogance and the jagged pinnacles of our selfishness, our many lusts for power, and our fear. The waves of his fury smashed themselves on the rocks below me, and drenched me with their spray.

I wiped the spume from my eyes and looked out to sea. Far, far out a bird moved over the waters, small, very small, dark above, white below, sharp pointed wings skimming the surface. It moved easily in the face of the storm, swinging from one trough to another, easily, easily, its wings never flapping, but tipping from side to side, almost touching the black water. Easily, easily it flew, and soon it had disappeared from my sight.

Thus the most graceful glory of God passed me by, as once it had passed by Moses hidden in a cleft of the rock of Sinai.[13] As it went, I heard above the waves' roaring its thin call. I tell you, it came to me like the cry of an unloved child.

I knew then that I was drenched not only by the flood of God's anger, but by the water of her tears.

❦9 The Tower[14]

To the people who lived there it was flat, grey, drab. The other creatures who inhabited the plain did not mind it. They thought there was nothing wrong with the place. But then they had always lived there, ever since the place had been a place. The people had moved into it from somewhere behind memory and had tried to make it their own.

They found belonging there difficult. They found being content there impossible. The whole area was just flat, grey and drab. There was nothing to lift the spirits, and no easy mastery either. The soil was hard to work, and kept its fertility for thorns and thistles. The rains could not be depended upon, and the whole region provided only two perpetual springs. They tried to make the place belong to them, but it remained intractable, and the more they tried, the less they seemed to belong.

Whatever they did, the plain remained flat, grey and interminably drab. There was nothing they saw or heard or felt or smelled or touched to lift their spirits. They could, of course, have raised their eyes to the vast sky, or sat at the feet of the other creatures who lived there and learned from them how to belong.

But they did neither, and so their discontent grew, and after a time turned into conflict. Not recognising the roots of their bitterness, they turned to distrusting, then hating, then fighting, one another. Unable to master the place, they tried to master their neighbours.

The fighting became centred, not surprisingly, around the two springs, the two places where life was more reliable, and where the greyness of the plain was dressed in green, and something rich and lush was to be found in all the drabness. For centuries the villages of the plain had regarded the springs as their common property, and had taken it in turns to till the fields around them and store their large yields. Irrigation channels had been extending slowly across the land, enlarging the green, breaking the flatness with the ridges of their banks, providing new hunting grounds for the heron and the snipe.

Now the springs that had been bringing life to the plain became centres of death. Each village claimed possession of one or the other of them, and when its claim went unheeded or was dismissed, it gave up words and beat its ploughshares into swords. The water of the springs was turned into blood, the banks of the irrigation channels slowly collapsed, and the plain resumed its dead flatness and laid aside its green.

Eventually the people had no more energy for fighting, and sank into a flaccid hatred. So it continued for centuries, till they quite forgot why they hated one another and only knew that they did.

Then one day someone in one of the villages learned how to make bricks and, having made lots of bricks, showed the people her vision. She took her index finger round the villages and drew her dream on the ground. She drew a tower with its top in the heavens and, for the first time, when the people raised their eyes from her drawing, they noticed the vastness of the sky.

For the first time for centuries something stirred the dark waters of their spirits and, indeed, it was very good. For the first time in the history of the plain the people of the villages met to do something together other than fight.

As the tower grew, so did their ambition. The sky seemed larger than ever, and they felt they could never touch it, until the maker of bricks, their architect, said, 'Why don't we build a spire on the top?' So they strengthened the walls of the tower and braced them with iron, and moved in a series of lesser spires from the square to the octagonal, and then climbed slowly upwards till they met together at the spire's crown and found themselves in heaven. And God looked up at their work and split heaven open with a cry of triumph. He had not felt such delight since he had made the world!

The people of the town round the base of the tower (for they had deserted their villages and had come to live together, bound by the common task, the shared vision) held a day of great celebration. They walked together a mile away across the plain, then as one they turned and saw what they had done. No longer was the place just flat, nor was it drab now. Against the plain's own loveliness, seen for the first time, and the awesome beauty of that huge sky, the spire astonished them.

The brick-maker had prepared a speech, but she did not deliver it. Like the rest she could not speak. In silence the people returned to the tower, and there they crowded into the bottom of it and listened as the brick-maker took up her lyre and played and sang. As she did so, the morning stars sang together and the sons of God shouted for joy[15] until God said to them, 'Be quiet! I'm listening!' and a great silence fell over the heavens.

Of course, the tower and spire are in ruins now. The bricks lie in heaps and are buried beneath the soil. Thick bushes have grown where once the brick-maker played, and the villages have withdrawn into their old sullenness. But I tell you this. In one of the bushes where the tower and spire stood a pair of nightingales have begun to nest. And I tell you another thing. The brick-maker, so they say, is not dead.

❦*10* The Risk[16]

'I have a few questions for you, Abraham. I do not expect you to answer.

'Was it because you were so numb with the shock of the divine command that you upped and went so readily?

'You went from Haran just like that, but then you did not have your son with you, nor that bundle of firewood. You did not take such care then to put your knife in your belt, or carry a flame to light the wood.

'When you went from Haran families were on the move all over the east, leaving their countries and their kindred and their fathers' houses. To join their journeyings must have cost you dear, Abraham, but there was nothing un-usual in it, nothing so very strange, except that you took with you all the promises of God and his plans for the world's redemption.

'But that other journey, that three-day slow plod of the ass to the land of Moriah, how could you have taken that, unless numb with shock? Did you not notice on the way how very still the land was? Did you not notice how the birds ceased their singing, how the eagles and the buz-zards broke from the circles of their soaring and hung in the air? Did you notice there were no sparrows, no larks scurrying across the face of the desert? Did you see them hiding in the shadows of the rocks, as motionless as the geckos and the lizards? No insects danced for you on the way, and the flowers furled their petals as you passed. All creation held its breath for you, Abraham. Were you blind and deaf to that? Did you just go on doggedly, looking neither right nor left, refusing to feel the silence, not daring to feel the pain, not bringing yourself to feel anything at all?

'Surely, Abraham, if you had stopped to think, you would have stopped, and turned back, and taken your son and the wood and the fire and the knife and the promises and purposes of God back home, to safety?

'You stopped to think in Egypt and in Gerar and everywhere else you went, when you told them Sarah was your sister.[17] You realised the risks then, at least the risks to yourself, and you were quick to avoid them. You were cunning then, resourceful, ruthless, decisive, quick to take matters into your own hands. Your cowardice then was clear, Abraham. So where did you find the courage, if that is what it was, to go to the land of Moriah with your son, your only son, the son whom you loved, Isaac? I do not understand it. Before he was born you laughed in God's face and thought him a fool. Why then, once he was born and weaned and old enough for a three-day journey, did you not think God ridiculous when he told you to cut the boy's throat and burn him to nothing? What made you recognise his deadly seriousness? One thing is for sure. You did not know how it would end. The mountain you were shown, the place where stone by stone you built the altar for your son, and carefully prepared his funeral pyre, was not called 'The Lord Provides' then, not at the beginning. You did not know, at the beginning. The sound of a ram's horn only reached your ears when it was nearly all over.

'And what of Sarah? What, indeed, of Sarah?! On the way, did you think of what you would say to her when you got back with the servants and the ass and the knife? Did you imagine to yourself how you would take her hand and try to look her in the eye and tell her you had killed her son? Did you work out a speech?

'Above all, Abraham, did you stop to think of the risk God was taking? Did you realise that if the knife had fallen, if Isaac's throat had been cut, if the smoke and the smell of his burning had filled God's nostrils, then all would have been lost? It would have been the end of everything. You would have cut the throat of Hope, and burned Love's desires to ashes. Though God had promised never again to flood the earth, it would, if your knife had fallen, have been washed away by his tears. There would have been no gospel left to proclaim, no space for the kingdom of God. All would have been drowned.

'These are my questions, Abraham. I do not expect you to answer.'

Abraham was silent for a time. Then he replied, 'I cannot answer your questions. You must do that. But I will tell you of another journey. They did not need to go nearly so far, only outside the city walls. It was not my son, and the altar was made of wood. But again all creation held its breath, and I could hear its heart beating in its fear. That time the knife fell, and the blood was spilled. There was no thicket there, no ram. It was like the Flood, perhaps. It marked the End of everything, and God had most certainly risked it all. And do you know what I call that place? "The Lord Provides". '

❧ 11 God's Sensuality

God sat in the wilderness, wondering. The wind blew the rainbow from her hair, and the vultures, not recognising, circled slowly in the sky above her, waiting for her death. In her cupped hand she held a scorpion, and to that small, intricate creature she poured out her soul.[18]

'I had a garden once,' she said, 'not far from here. It went to rack and ruin long ago. I used to walk there in the cool of the day,[19] with the stars in my hair and the dew of creation on my feet. He came to me every day, beneath the tree in the middle of the garden. Every day we met there. Every day. I have not always been here, you see, out here in the wilderness. It used to be far easier, far more natural. We used to sing love songs to one another. He loved me then. He called me his "sister", his "bride", and I could call him "my love". I excited him then, so he said. Listen, scorpion, and I will tell you one of the songs he sang to me:

> "With one flash of your eyes, you excite me.
> One jewel on your neck stirs my heart,
>> O my sister, my bride.
>
> Your love, more than wine, is enticing,
> Your fragrance is finer than spices,
>> My sister, my bride.
>
> Your lips, sweet with nectar, invite me
> To honey and milk on your tongue,
>> O my sister, my bride.
>
> And even your clothing is fragrant
> As wind from the Lebanon mountains,
>> My sister, my bride."[20]

'We understood one another then. He does not sing to me any more, not that song, not a song like that. He has turned me into a concept, a thing to argue over. He has made me difficult. I have become the plaything of his clever mind. He has forgotten my sensuality. And that is why I am out here in the wilderness. He has forgotten my sensuality. You can, of course, embrace a concept. But it is a cold embrace. It doesn't do much for you. It won't keep you warm at night. And you cannot sing to it, not a song like that. He has forgotten my sensuality,' she said.

The scorpion twitched uneasily, and she set the creature down on the ground. It scampered off. She bent down and drew with her finger on the ground. Then she looked up at the vultures weaving a shroud for her in the sky. She laughed. 'Stupid birds!' she said, and walked over to where the scapegoat was standing.[21] She put her arm round the goat's neck. 'So it's you and me on our own again, is it, you, me and the desert wind? But we make a fine trio!'

With that she jumped lightly on to the scapegoat's back, and began to ride across the hard rock, with the wind blowing the rainbow from her hair, and the perfumes of Eden streaming from her clothes. 'I will remind him,' she said to herself, and then tossing her head back she cried to the vultures, 'I am not dead yet!' The birds recognised her voice, and the bare skin on their necks blushed bright red in the evening sun as they rose to hide their faces in the clouds.

'I am not dead yet!' and she laughed, and rode on towards the edge of the desert.

She could see a small figure walking slowly out to meet her. 'What are you doing here, Elijah?' she said.[22]

'*You* may not be dead, but I am, nearly.'

'But what are you doing here?'

'I have come to complain.'

'I thought so. You haven't come to love me, by any chance? What do you think of my hair?'

'I have come to complain. You made it mighty difficult for me, hiding yourself away in this wretched place. But that's not what I came to complain about.'

'Do you want a ride? It's not very comfortable, riding the scapegoat, but it's the best we can do.'

'I came to say . . .'

God interrupted him. 'It's no good, Elijah. You don't complain properly, not like Job. Your complaints are heavy with your own ambition.[23] You want to wrap me round your little finger. That's no good. Job was different. He let me embrace him, you see. I can't touch you, Elijah.' She looked away, and started to ride on.

Elijah gazed after her, not seeing very well. 'But if you jump up on the goat's back,' she called back, 'I'll hold you tight so you don't fall.'

The prophet did not know what to do. He turned, stopped, shook himself, turned again. Then the wind took her scent to him and caught him.

'I have you by the nose, Elijah!' and she split the rock with her delight, and sent streams of laughter flowing over the sand. 'You can come out of the clouds now!' she yelled to the vultures.

She offered him her hand and swung him up on to the goat's back in front of her. They swayed uneasily as the goat picked its way down from the dry plateau towards the fields, but once on the smooth road among the orange groves Elijah's waist relaxed in her grip, and he moved to the rhythm of her song:

> 'Stamp me in your heart,
> Upon your limbs,
> Sear my emblem deep
> into your skin.

> For love is strong as death,
> Harsh as the grave.
> Its tongues are flames, a fierce
> And holy blaze.
>
> Endless seas and floods,
> Torrents and rivers
> Never put out love's
> Infinite fires.'[24]

They rode into the city together. 'Why should she speak of death in a love song?' he wondered. Then, as the crowds greeted them with their branches of palm,[25] he remembered.

🎋 12 God's Passion[26]

Now the word of the Lord came to Jonah ben Amittai, saying, 'Arise, go to my garden, and I will meet you there in the cool of the day.' So Jonah arose, and this time he did as he was told, and went to Eden, where he played with the animals (all duly named). Then, feeling tired, he went to sleep beneath the tree in the middle of the garden.

God came to him and nudged him out of his siesta, and said, 'It is time we understood one another, you and I.' Jonah opened an eye, and got the shock of his life. There before him, so it seemed, was a young woman. She said, 'You, Jonah, come from the heart of my desire. You are bone of my bone, and flesh of my flesh. I have always loved you. You have spent your life avoiding me, but now here you are in my garden. We are alone together you and I. It is time we understood one another.' And she kissed him.

Jonah said nothing. In the farthest recesses of his memory he remembered the kiss that had brought the first man to life on the same spot of ground in Eden, but he could not believe his ears, and he could not believe his lips either. God looked at him and cried, 'Now you will not believe your finger!' and she laughed. Before Jonah realised what was happening, she got out a prayer book and put two rings in the palm of her hand. 'We do not need a priest,' she said. 'I will be your priest, and you will be mine.' She began to read. The words danced a jig in the air of the garden. Jonah in his bewilderment and great astonishment found it hard to catch them, but faintly he heard himself saying, 'I take you to be my wife, to have and to hold from this day forward; for better, for worse, for richer, for poorer, in sickness and in health, to love and to cherish,' and he heard those words repeated exactly, except that 'wife' became 'husband', and when he looked at his hand there was a ring on his finger that shone with all the colours of the first rainbow, and between his forefinger and thumb was another ring that was exactly the same. A hand was stretched out towards his, a left hand with its third finger extended, and, before he knew it, he had slipped the second ring upon it.

'Now you may kiss the bride,' she said. The sun above the garden went down, night fell, and the animals left Jonah and his bride to their new joy.

Next morning God said to Jonah, 'Now we understand one another, you and I.' Jonah believed her. Yet Jonah had not reckoned with God's ambition. She had come as a surprise to him, to put it mildly, but now he thought he knew where he stood. No more going off to Tarshish and getting wet. No more smelling of fish. He could stay in the garden with God and till it and keep it, and grow leeks and chrysanthemums, and, what with his wife's know-how, win first prize every time at the local flower and vegetable show, wherever that was. So it came as a shock, to put it mildly, when she squeezed his hand one night and spoke of going to Nineveh. It was not merely that going to Nineveh was inconvenient. It was unthinkable. It lay beyond Jonah's wildest imaginings. So he chose not to imagine it, but ordered several loads of bricks instead, and started building a wall round Eden.

Thus it was that God had to find her way to Nineveh on her own. Nineveh, however, was a very wicked city.[27] Everyone knows that. It was no place for a woman on her own.

49

🐍 *13* God's Love Song[28]

Behind the cliffs the rough grassland and scrub rose to a sharp ridge. From the top the views would surely be immense. At the highest point three small trees grew, bent double by the sea wind. Two hundred feet below me the high waves curled and broke against the cliffs. The air was noisy with the cries of kittiwakes. Fulmars glided past, following the contours of the cliff, almost touching the rock with the tips of their wings. Out to sea, gannets wheeled in tight circles, dazzling white as they turned in the sun and, suddenly twisting, dived one after another upon a shoal of fish. A flock of guillemots exploded from the foot of the cliffs and flew pellmell over the water, as if all the world was after them. Immediately below me on a low rock a razorbill attempted to mount its mate, missed, and fell into the sea.

The air was warm and lazy, but I turned and made briskly for the ridge. The sound of the kittiwakes receded, to be replaced by the singing of larks. There was no path, and near the top the ground was surprisingly steep. I fell to climbing on my hands and knees. I looked up to check my bearings. The three trees were above me, a little to my left. I did not see her then, but only the trees' shade. I made as straight as I could for that. At last the ground began to level off and, panting hard, I straightened up. The trees were only a few yards away now, and there she was, sitting beneath the middle one, watching me. She wore the stars of the Pleiades and Orion in her hair and a hundred rainbows danced about her limbs. The skin of her face shone bright in the shadow of the tree, and her eyes were as deep at the ocean. She looked at me and smiled. 'Come over here,' she said quietly, 'and rest beside me in the shade.'

I did not know where to put myself. I had come up on to the ridge for the view, the panorama, the sea and the cliffs curving round towards that nice town in the bay and the fields stretching inland. I had wanted to know if you could see the gap in the second, higher ridge to the north, and the ruins of the castle on its great mound that almost filled it. I had come for a bit of a sit-down and a few sandwiches and a cup of tea from the thermos and a chance to take it all in, so as I could say when I got home that, yes, I'd had a nice day, thank you, and wasn't it lovely and warm for the time of year, because June is so often disappointing, isn't it? I had not climbed up from the cliff path for this, not for her. I did not know what to do. Should I say something? But what should I say? What can you say in such a situation? Should I offer her a sandwich? I looked down towards the cliffs, and started taking off my rucksack. But I stopped with one of the straps still over my shoulder, for behind my back she started singing gently.

Her song took up the rhythms of the sea, wove them together with the singing of the larks and the cries of the gulls, then, expanding, took all the beauty of the world and all love's longing and gave them to me in its melody. She was singing a love song. She was singing it for me! I turned round to look at her, but she had gone.

The sandwiches were untouched when I got home, and the thermos unopened.

*　　*　　*

Ever since then I have been searching to hear that song again. Sometimes I think I hear it, and in the most

51

unlikely places too, but it is usually very faint. We make so much noise, you see. But I cannot get it out of my head. And one more thing I know: her song is never finished. It is not that she has stopped singing. Just that I do not hear it. We make too much noise, keep ourselves too busy and our expectations too mundane. That is what I think, anyway.

I wish I could sing like that.

❧14 God's Mountain²⁹

It was indeed an awe-inspiring sight. It rose dark and threatening out of the desert, its top many thousands of feet above the surrounding plain, and shrouded always in mist. The holy mountain of God. The mountain where once before, so the story went, God had met his people, the place where surely he would come to them again. The signs were there. A strange light had appeared in the sky, like a pillar of fire, seeming to want to draw people in its wake towards the mountain. Eagles, buzzards and falcons had been seen weaving strange patterns in the sky. Kings were on the move in distant lands, and local shepherds were getting restless.

The signs were there, and people looked out for signs then. The pillar of fire, the birds, the kings and shepherds did not go unnoticed. The desert was no longer deserted, but became a huge metropolis as a great mass of people converged on the mountain from all directions. They came in their thousands, in their hundreds of thousands, in the end in their millions, almost all of them on foot. There were bands of young men laughing and joking, each trying to give the impression he did not mind the heat and the dust and the weariness of the place. There were small children, for whom this was a great adventure, who really did not mind the heat and the dust, or else were asleep, riding on their fathers' shoulders. There were babies being carried by their mothers, and behind them all the old, the blind and the lame, and a few heavily pregnant women stumbling, gasping in the heat, but still going on, drawn like everyone else to the great surge of rock ahead of them. The rich came on their camels, and the poor came also, their feet bound with cloth to protect them from the heat of the sand and the sharp stones. Saints and holy women and men came together with the godless and the wicked. Ruthlessness and cruelty were among them, and greed, lust and hatred. Love was there in all its fierceness, with faith and hope, along with gentleness, kindness and fine humility. Many joys came to that mountain, many sadnesses too, and much grief. All travelled to the one mountain and for one purpose.

Not everyone was sure that that purpose would be fulfilled. Perhaps God would not make an appearance this time. Perhaps the signs were not signs at all. Perhaps, after all, at the end of the journey everything signified nothing. Yet no one was utterly certain he would not come. All had their hopes, even if they would not admit to them.

The mountain held them all in its spell, and one more thing united them: the great weariness of the desert. As they reached the foot of the mountain they sank down on the rock, exhausted, and the desert larks and the white-crowned wheatears ran among their bodies. Nobody dared venture on the slopes above. It was God's mountain, not theirs. Even the wicked and the insane sensed that. They camped at its foot, and waited. What for exactly, they did not know. What would the coming of God be like? They did not know. But they were sure there would be lightning and thunder, a few mysterious trumpet blasts maybe, and no doubt the ground would shake and the mountain would tremble and smoke and burn with fire.

That is what they expected. So, soon after the sun had gone down behind the mountain, making the mist on top seem like the smoke of a great fire, it came as no surprise when a violent storm suddenly broke upon them. They huddled together, drawing their cloaks about their shoulders and around the quivering bodies of their children. The vast black sides of the mountain bent over them. They were dwarfed by them, made to feel as nothing, and at the height of the storm it seemed they might with one last awful crash of thunder split and crack down upon them and become their burial mound. Yet in the midst of their terror they still waited, listening for the voice of their God in the howl of the wind and the roar of the thunder. For surely he had come to his mountain in this storm, and surely he would speak to them again as he had done through his servant Moses all those centuries before.

But no voice came. Only the wind and the lightning and the thunder. Perhaps after the storm? Yes, that was it! After the storm! When, at dawn the next day, the storm subsided as suddenly as it had begun, all eyes turned towards the summit. The mist had lifted. The very peak of the mountain could be seen, not black and menacing, but shining gold and pink in the first rays of the new sun. Then it was that God came to his mountain. Then it was, in the deep silence of that dawn, that God spoke to his people. But not from the summit. That lifting of the eternal mist and the exquisite shining of the peak, that was a mere jest of his. No, he spoke from among them, from their very midst, down there on the plain at the mountain's foot. Just as the storm ended, in the middle of that great mass of people, a young woman gave birth to a baby, a son, and in the silence of the dawn the child uttered its first cry.

God had spoken. Emmanuel.

❦15 God's Tears

She was over ninety, but had the spirit of a nineteen-year-old and the mischief of a boy of eight. She had known misery in her time, of course, but to be with her was to find a laughter that was larger than any grief and that could wipe away all tears. She had, more conspicuously than anyone else I had ever known, met God.

'How did you find him?' I asked her one day.

'In the holy city,' she replied, 'in the palace at its centre – but not where I expected. It was not at all what I expected, not at all.'

'Go on,' I said.

'Yes. Well, I was walking in the holy city one day, as one does, you know, the new Jerusalem and all that – at least, I thought that's where I was – and I came to its very centre, to a vast golden palace. As I stood watching the birds tumbling about its pinnacles, a great procession came round the corner and advanced towards the gates. There were angels and archangels and cherubim and seraphim and all the razzmatazz of heaven! But God was not in the procession.

'Caught up in the crowd, I went inside the palace, and found myself with all those angels and archangels and cherubim and seraphim in a gleaming throne room. The throne itself was huge! It took up the whole of the end wall, and upon it was light, the light, you might have thought, of the burning bush, the light of the light of the world. But God was not in the light.

'I slipped out of a side door, and was alone in another, even larger, room. You could have put two cathedrals in it quite easily, with room still to spare. Far above my head was a great dome, and painted on that dome, and filling it entirely, was a severe, frowning face. Far above me it was, yet the frown was inside me, too, accusing me. Beneath it, possessing it, I felt so very small, so foolish, so awkward, so inadequate, so guilty, so alone. But God was not in the frown.

'Lost and bewildered, I didn't know where to go next. Then I heard a faint crying and, clutching on to its sound, I threaded my way along it through the labyrinth of the palace until I was climbing up bare attic stairs and opening a door on to a small, dingy room. On a pile of sacking in the corner was a baby, crying, alone. In his tears all the misery of the world was distilled. His cheeks were stained with all the anguish of the bereaved, all the pain of those who are made to feel small or stupid. All the hurt of the bullied, the despised, the abused and the friendless was caught between the walls of that room. All the agony of God was in the crying.

'So I picked my God up from his pile of sacking, and I wiped his tears and held him close to me and carried him with all the weight of that sorrow down the stairs and along the corridors of the palace, through the space with the frowning dome, until I reached the throne room and its huge throne that took up the whole of the end wall. In my arms my God had stopped crying, and so I laid him gently on the throne, and stepped back to look at him. He was quiet now and still. He looked so funny, lying so tiny on that vast throne. He heard me laugh, and turned his face towards me and giggled. And in that giggle was all God's glee and all the world's joy.

'That is our task,' she said, 'yours and mine: to take God up in our arms and hold him tight and wipe away his tears, that we might make him laugh again. Then we will know what joy is.' She laughed.

❧ 16 God's Mischief

When the Lord God was very small he liked to ride round his garden on a tiger. One day they came to the edge of the garden, and were surprised to find a high wall there. In the middle of the wall was an iron door. The tiger bent his head against it and pushed, but try as he might, despite his great strength, he could not open it. So the Lord God fell off his back on to the grass, crawled up to the door, placed his small hand upon it and swung it open. They passed through it together.

The other side was a vast space, enclosed on all sides by the same high wall, and in the middle of the space was a strange, tangled, intricate, louring, soaring edifice. Its top reached to the heavens, and round its base people walked admiringly. Others lay stretched out on the ground, resting in its shade, hid themselves in its dark crevices, or gathered in groups in its many passages. Some were shouting loudly from its roof-tops. Yet others sat beneath it weeping, or else twitched and writhed, impaled upon its pinnacles.

The tiger walked his graceful walk around it with his God once more on his back. 'What could it be?' he wondered to himself. But the child God knew the many names it bore. Some called it 'The State', others 'The People', or 'The Company', or 'The Faith'.

'Go back to the garden,' God whispered, 'and shut the door behind you.' He then slid down the tiger's tail on to the ground. The animal flicked his ears, turned, and went home. God watched him go, then began to crawl towards one of the corners of the building. It was most wonderfully made. Some of its edges were jagged and dark with blood, but its pretensions were as bright as ever. It rested on four slender pillars, which curved inwards towards the centre, like flying buttresses on a cathedral. No one noticed him, and eventually the child God reached one of the pillars, and put his small hand upon it. He pushed.

*　　*　　*

When God was a boy he liked to slide down the banisters of the galaxies, or play with the silent creatures at the bottom of the ocean. But one afternoon he was doing neither. He was bored. He lay on his front, drawing pictures in the dust. Far below him self-important men in long black robes led smart, uncomfortable people to their places in rows of uncomfortable chairs. A table was set ready, with white linen upon it, and a little way behind that was a large chair in awkward isolation. An organ played. From time to time the Lord God looked down at the people shifting on their seats. But he spent more time looking through the window beside him. Outside the porch of the cathedral a young woman stood with a small girl at her side. Her God could see the frown of her face, and could catch the sharp edge to her voice and its hidden fear, as she asked those going inside if they might give her and her child some money for food.

The service began, but the Lord God hardly noticed. It had begun to rain heavily, and he watched through the window as the woman and her child slipped into the porch, and was still watching when they emerged again and were waved away by one of the men in black. He heard the words of his dismissal. 'This is a house of God,' he said to them, thinking it an adequate explanation. 'And there's an important service going on,' he added when they did not move away. That seemed sufficient, so he went back inside, out of the rain.

The service continued, but still God watched out of the window. Had the woman received too many rebuffs like that? How much spirit had she left inside her? Would she do as she was told? No! He saw her wait a while, then slip in another door that was not so well guarded. Looking down inside the nave, he saw the pair of them quickly find two chairs at the side, near the back, beside the tomb of a very reverend and very dead bishop. God clapped his hands and laughed. His timing was unfortunate. The uncomfortable people had got to a particularly quiet moment in the prayers. A thousand pairs of eyes looked up at the triforium. But God slipped behind a pillar just in time, and the men in black decided it must have been one of 'those blasted pigeons'.

The service went on and on, and God began to fidget. He took his service sheet in his hands and started to fold it. He was, as you might expect, very good at origami. The paper took the shape not of an aeroplane, but of a dove. He was pleased with his work. 'Very good,' he said to himself, and a wicked grin spread across his face.

The service approached its climax. Far below a man knelt down before the great chair. The great man on the great chair leant forward. A group of other men, all scarlet, black and white, approached the kneeling figure and surrounded him with their splendour. Hands were laid upon his head, or stretched out towards it. The archbishop opened his mouth to speak splendid words, but then a gasp went up from the congregation as a dove descended from on high. It flew straight for the head of the kneeling man! Yet at the last second it swerved and hit the top of the archbishop's mitre, sending it tumbling on to the floor. From the triforium came a boyish and God-like yell of pure delight, and from the west end came a raucous and most discourteous laugh.

After hearing this, you will not be surprised to learn that when God grew to be a man, they crucified him.

❧ 17 The Scapegoat

The stadium was full to bursting. In the middle of the green space was a stage covered by an awning, and in the centre of the stage sat the holy man whom all had come to see. He was dressed simply, in white, not enthroned on a grand chair, but sitting cross-legged on a carpet. He spoke in words that all could understand, and the thousands in the stadium hung on to every one of them. He is like a god, I thought, and there was hardly anyone there who thought otherwise.

'I must speak with him,' I said to myself. 'I must see him and speak to him face to face.' And indeed the very next day I did.

He lived in a palace, in the servants' quarters. In a small, plain room at the top of the building I talked with him face to face, as a man speaks to his friend.[30] I poured out my soul to him. He listened with a serene smile upon his face, and even before he had spoken I had fallen under his spell. I went back down the servants' stairs feeling like a god myself. I had found peace, I thought, and contentment. Nothing troubled that old man's face. It seemed that nothing had ever troubled it, or ever could. He was at ease, profoundly at ease, and when I had given him all my longings, he had promised the earth in return.

'You are my child,' he had said, 'but I, your father, will be your slave. I will make a highway for you in your desert. I will lift up every valley for you, and all your mountains and hills will be made low. The uneven ground shall become level for you, and the rough places a plain, and all shall see my glory and yours.'[31]

'You are my child, and I, your father, will be your slave. Seek from me, and you will find. Knock on my door, and always it shall be opened to you.[32] I will grant you power, and all things will be well. I will give you success, and health and length of days. All your schemes will prosper, for I, your father, love you and intend that all things for you should be well.

'If only more people would seek audience with me, as you have done today. If only more would let me serve them. If only more would fall under my spell. Then they might share in your joy, have a taste of your power, and know the peace that you most surely will find.'

Oh, I have so many stories to tell of the years after that hour with the holy man in his attic room at the top of the servants' stairs. He was right. All things were well, it seemed. My schemes prospered, my health was strong, my days became long, and those who knew me envied me my peace and serenity.

Others, many, many others, went to the holy man as I had done, and found what I had found, and came to tell much the same stories as I did. When, therefore, ten years later he came again to the city to speak to the people in the stadium, there were tens of thousands upon tens of thousands there to hear him, and when he came and sat down upon the carpet in the centre of the stage and a great silence fell, waiting for him to begin, I shouted at the top of my voice, 'My Lord and my God!', and tens of thousands upon tens of thousands took up the cry, and thousands more still outside the stadium heard the shout and begged the police to open another gate and let them in, that they might worship him also.

So a gate was opened, and one hundred people died in the crush, and hundreds more were injured, and when I looked to see where my Lord and my God was, he was nowhere to be seen.

I left the city then, without my power, without my joy and my peace. I turned my back on the palace and went instead into the wilderness, to live among the desert larks and the ibex.

I saw not another soul, until one day I met a man leading a ragged goat down to a stream gushing out of a rock. He was dressed simply, in white. Or rather, it had once been white; now it was stained with the dust of the desert and spattered, I thought, with blood. As I drank from the water from the rock, he patted the neck of his companion and said, 'The scapegoat and I keep one another company. We understand each other.'[33]

He was silent for a long time. Then he turned to me and looked me deep in the eye. 'On that terrible day in the stadium you lost your god. He melted away in the crowd. He could do no more there. He went far away, to another city. He preaches there now, to tens of thousands upon tens of thousands. He is doing very well. Will you now follow me?'

He paused for my answer. None came. He paused still. Still none came.

With quiet urgency he spoke again. 'I cannot promise you the same kind of power or success, nor the same joy or peace. For with me and the scapegoat here you will have to surrender your self-centredness. I will wash your feet and be your slave,[34] but I will do that because I choose to do so, and because in truth I love you, not because you have me on your chain or that I wish to have you on mine. And if I wash your feet, then I will wash the feet of all, whether they pay me homage or not. It will be long and tiring work. There are many feet in the world, and they are all tired and sore, and some will kick you in

the face for your trouble. See, I have no teeth left at all!'
and he grinned up at me.

'Come with me, and I will promise you nothing but a
fierce love that will never let you go. That is all. At times it
will be enough, and at those times you will glimpse the
kingdom of God. A fierce love, that is all, and my tears
and my anger and my grin. The scapegoat never leaves my
side. Will you come with me also? We will have such
times together! Such times, such times!'

He got up, put his hand on the neck of the goat, and
slowly they began to walk away, towards the city and its
empty stadium.

The first time it happened it was marvellous! Everyone said it was the best wedding for years. The party went on well into the night and all the guests wanted to know the name of the wine and its vintage.

'The waters of Eden must have tasted like this!' someone said.

'Or that sparkling water with a hint of bitter herbs that came from the rock in the wilderness!'[36] said another.

'Or the wine of that wedding feast on Sinai when God took us for his bride!' cried a third.

But none of them knew the name of the wine, and the vintage was as old as the hills and far older.

And the earth woke from her slumber and laughed, and the whale slapped the ocean on the back with her fluke, and the bees danced and the tiger purred loud and deep and the nightingale took up the instrument of his soul and sang in the dark wood.

The second time it happened it was 'too good, far too good to be true!' they said. They had thought it would not happen again, but here it was in front of them, down their throats, warming their stomachs, the same wine all over again, as old as the hills and far older, and as red and as deep as the blood of a god. Perhaps heaven had come to stay, not just for the weekend, but for ever! A pattern in things seemed to be emerging. Perhaps this was how it would always be, this joy, this generosity, this to-hell-with-the-expense-devil-may-care prodigality!

And the earth laughed again and the whale slapped the ocean's back with her fluke and the bees danced and the tiger purred loud and deep, and in the dark wood the nightingale took up the instrument of his soul and sang.

When it happened a third time, it was, frankly, beginning to be embarrassing. Oh, some were not the slightest bit embarrassed. They had come to the wedding feast with their own buckets of water and had sat beside them, tongues lolling, waiting for the transformation. They were not at all embarrassed, but they were very angry when others had so much of the wine and they had none. Yet those others, those fortunate ones, were left discomfited. It was unnerving, to say the least. There was something subversive about this wild extravagance. They caught a whiff of danger in the air.

Yet still the earth laughed and the whale slapped the ocean on the back and the bees danced and the tiger purred loud and deep and the nightingale sang in the dark wood.

Come the sixth and the seventh and the tenth and the twentieth wedding in the town when water was turned into wine, that same wine, as old as the hills and far older and as red and as deep as the blood of a god, there was positive alarm. The wine merchants could see themselves going out of business if it went on much longer. But the black waters of fear spread wider than that, and dripped into deep caverns of the mind. It *was* dangerous, this to-hell-with-the-expense-devil-may-care prodigality, this strange generosity, this wild extravagance. It *was* disorderly. It did not obey the rules. It showed no proper respect of persons. Those who tried with their buckets of water to manipulate it through their greed got nowhere. That, perhaps, was not so very surprising. But it seemed it could not be controlled at all. It could not be brought to heel. It could not be made safe. No ring could be put through its nose. It would roam free, wherever it wished, dangerous, enormously strong, its own master, a veritable god in the wide land.

So they drove the wine-maker out of the town, and lived on in safety without him.

'What happened to him?' you may ask. 'Did he die alone under a hedge one cold winter's night?'

Oh no. He went to share the earth's glee, to ride on the broad back of the whale, to dance with the bees. He found warm lodging in the tiger's throat, and in the dark wood he took up the instrument of his soul and sang duets with the nightingale.

❧ 19 The Grass-eater³⁷

Passing over the great, hot plains, I saw in the picture developing in the dark room of my mind a pride of lions, sprawled on the rock, lazily, in the shade of the trees. In my picture I was too close to make a run for it. I had no gun, no companion, no jeep. How I had got there I do not know, but there I was, in the middle of nowhere, fifteen yards from a pride of lions.

They seemed to me to be asleep, but, as I stood and stared, they watched me, and one old lion slowly raised himself and started padding towards me. Strangely I felt no fear. He came right up to me, that rather battered-looking lion, and led me to the rock where the other lions and lionesses were waiting, and showed me a place where I might sit among them. I sat down.

They looked at me with a strange look I had not seen before. It was not frightening. In fact, it took away any traces of fear left in me. After a while I lowered my eyes, feeling unworthy of their gaze. Then it was that the old lion spoke, and this is what, in my imagining, he said.

'The far side of this great plain, near the mountains where the sun rises, there was an age ago a large pride of lions, and among them a great king among lions, whose like had never been seen before. You would not have picked him out from a distance. He was not the largest of the pride, nor the most handsome. But when you got close to him, you sensed he was not like the rest. You felt he understood things the rest of us did not, and saw things in a different way. I grew up with him in the same pride, and we learned the skills of hunting together.

'For many years he bided his time, waiting in the shadows of the pride, till one hot day when we surprised a large herd of zebra. Two of our largest lionesses were doing most of the running as usual, and he was stationed to cut off the retreat of one of the weaker animals which might be separated from the rest of the herd. The lionesses worked beautifully! Soon they were driving their victim towards the place where he was supposed to be waiting in the tall grass. But he wasn't there!

'We eventually found him – we were angry because we had missed our zebra – lying the other side of some rocks, chewing grass! He smiled up at us. He almost laughed at us. In our astonishment we found nothing to say, and nothing to do, but go away suspicious and deeply afraid. At least, the others were afraid. I wasn't. I don't know why. I think I must have been expecting something like that to happen.

'Though the others were so frightened, they were content to hide their fear for a while, and it did not come to the surface until that stupid warthog came on the scene. Our strange lion had not been out hunting with us since the incident of the escaped zebra. He ate his wretched grass, and we left him alone. Even I left him alone. What would the rest have said, if I had stayed with him all day? But I tell you, I had little joy in the hunt or the kill in those days.

'One day we were sleeping under the trees, and Grass-eater was lying by himself not far off, when we were woken by the smell of warthog. Silly animal! I don't know whether its nose was blocked with dirt and it was practising walking with its eyes shut, but it came within forty yards of us before it stopped. The next instant it was flying in terror, with the whole lot of us beating behind it. In its path lay a huge mass of smooth rock, rising almost vertical out of the plain. The warthog could not hope to climb it, and we were gaining on it.

'Then I saw something flash past me twenty yards to my right. I have never seen a lion move as he did! I almost looked for dark lines on his cheeks and spots on his skin, to see if he had turned himself into a cheetah. It was the Grass-eater. Seeing him, the others were spurred on and leapt after him through the grass. Only I slackened my speed, and was suddenly afraid.

'I saw him reach the warthog, which was standing helpless beneath the cliff, with its back to the cold rock. And I saw him turn and face us as we came towards him, and his eyes were fierce, and he let out a roar such as none of us had heard before, a roar that made us stop, drop still in the tall grass. When eventually the roaring ceased, and in a huge silence we raised our heads, the warthog was gone, and he was slowly walking towards us, enquiring of us.

'The others hated him from that day, and began to see why he had made them so afraid before. You see, he was endangering the pride by his stupid antics (or so they thought), he was not being true to the lion in him (or so they thought). In the end it was his grass-eating that they loathed most of all, not his interfering in the hunt, but his chewing of that wretched silly grass! You see, he challenged their whole way of life, their whole philosophy, their whole world. With him around, they no longer knew where or who they were, and not to know that is a most terrible thing.

'He could have gone away altogether, I suppose, and left us to ourselves. But he didn't, and the end was inevitable. They plotted against him, and one day they turned on him, all of them, except for me and one or two others who had begun to feel as I did. They killed him, and ate his body, till he was nothing but bones for the vultures to pick at.

'We came away then, I and the others who felt as I did, and formed our own pride, the one that you see here.'

The old lion fell silent, and I watched his sadness. Hidden beneath it was something that was not sad at all, but I did not come to understand what it was until a few days later. You see, I remained with those lions for some time, and watched them and talked with them, as they lay chewing the tall grass. I became fascinated by the way they talked of that king among lions with the swiftness of the cheetah, and a taste for grass. It was almost as if . . .

Well, one afternoon I was sitting beside the old lion, when suddenly he sat up, his ears quivering.

'Listen!' he cried, 'Listen! Listen to his roaring! Come on, quickly!'

He sped off with the other lions across the plain. Of course, I could not hope to follow, so I watched, and then I saw it. Half a mile away another pride of lions was hunting a lone zebra. They almost had it surrounded. One of them had already drawn blood on its hind leg. In another moment they would have it, and would be tearing at its flesh, while its head lay flicking on the grass. But then there came the roar of a lion which seemed to fill the plain, and bounce back from the mountains at its edge. The hunters dropped down in the grass, and my lions (for I call them that now) reached the zebra and led him away through the grass, past the crouching figures, and back to where I was standing.

I understood then. As they lay there licking the zebra's wounded leg, speaking gently to him, I saw, reflected in their eyes, tiny, but quite distinct, the image of a strange lion, alone, walking through the tall grass, while behind him (I could just make it out) a warthog fled to safety. But what brought me my new understanding was not so much what I saw, as what I heard. It came from them, and yet it

72

did not come from them. It was far larger, far greater than they were. Filling the plain, rippling the blades of grass, vibrating through the ground beneath my feet, reverberating through the sky, and pulsating through the very stuff and fabric of this earth (or so it seemed to me in my imagining) was the unmistakable purr of a lion, the purr of the Grass-eater.

❧20 The Peregrine

We stood together on the cliff top, leaning on the stile in the delicious cool of the evening sun. To the west I could see a wedge-shaped headland, rising from almost nothing on the landward side to, well, it must be all of five hundred feet, before suddenly dropping sheer into the sea.

'That looks a fine place,' I said.

'It is that,' he replied. 'Fine place. Holy, too. At any rate, it is for me. Doesn't belong to anybody. Least ways it shouldn't. It's the peregrines' land, that is. It's their world, not ours, or it ought to be. Should be named after them. It isn't, of course.'

'What are peregrines?' I asked.

He looked at me. 'You've never seen peregrines?'

'I don't even know what they are.'

He looked at me again. 'They're birds,' he said. 'Falcons. Pointed wings, heavy bodies, black and white heads, grey-blue above, and *fast*. You think birds can fly till you see a peregrine up to its tricks. Then you know what flying is. You can keep your "Red Arrows", your Concordes, your Space Shuttles. Peregrines know what flying is.'

He paused, and I could see on his face the shadows of the pictures filling his mind. I waited.

'The first time I saw one on that headland, he was being mobbed by choughs and ravens,' he continued. 'I suppose you don't know what choughs or ravens are, either.'

'As a matter of fact, I do.'

He glanced at me in surprise. 'He shot straight upwards, out from the middle of them. Until then I didn't know any bird could fly vertically, straight up like that. But he did. The choughs and ravens didn't have a chance. They're well known for their acrobatics, but they couldn't touch that. Not straight up, and not at that speed.

'I saw them mobbing him again later. He did the same as before, only this time he twisted and turned as he went. It was getting on a bit by then, and he shone bright gold in the setting sun.

'I watched him on two other evenings. He wasn't the only peregrine on that headland. I saw him with one other bird first, then with two. He was teaching them to hunt. Playing with them. And playing with the air and the wind. They would soar in gentle circles, high up, mewing to one another (there's a sound for you!) and then they would tumble out of the sky and disappear. Once he did that, and a minute or so later shot up from below and passed directly over my head.

'He would float in the wind, twisting his tail to keep himself steady, and then he would turn and glide and half close his wings and be gone.

'Once, once I saw him very high up with one of the young ones. They were sitting on the wind, tails fanned, wings held stiff, not moving. I could only focus on one of them at a time. I saw him begin to slip, very gently, easily, slowly. I thought he would stop. I've often seen a kestrel hovering. That's another kind of falcon, smaller, not so powerful, not so fast – though they can move too, can kestrels. Spend a lot of time hovering, looking for things to catch on the ground beneath them. You must have seen them above the motorway verges. Anyway, as I was saying, I've often seen a kestrel shift its position a little, swing down just a few feet, perhaps, and start hovering again. I thought he, the peregrine, was going to do the same: just ease down twenty feet and stop. But he didn't. Suddenly he closed his wings and dropped. From where I was watching he seemed to come straight down. He went out of my sight behind a cliff. When I looked up for the other bird, that was gone, too. They had been playing with one another.'

He stopped, and for a moment or two I dared not disturb his memories.

'Have you seen him this year?'

'Yes.' He paused a long time. 'He's dead. There's a man lives on the headland, and likes to think he owns it. Likes to think he's the master there. He couldn't stand the peregrine. Came out one morning early, when there was no one about, and shot him. Went and picked him up, and took him – I know, because I saw him three days ago – and nailed him up in one of his outhouses. He put a nail through the end of each of his wings. Stretched out he was, like this.' He held out his arms wide.

Tears filled his eyes, and he looked away from the headland. He seemed not to hear the clear mewing of a peregrine falcon, riding high above our heads, calling to us.

৺ 21 The Calming of the Storm

It was finished.

Behind them in the far distance, three crosses could still be glimpsed on a low hill, if you knew where to look. They were hard to see against the background of the temple and the Roman garrison. They knew where to look only too well, but they did not turn round as they went over the top of the ridge. It was finished. There was no point in looking back. It was the scene not only of his death, but of their cowardice and desertion. No point in adding to their pain. They could only walk on, in mechanical fashion, as if they had already walked for miles and did not know how to stop. They said nothing to one another. There was no point. It was all finished.

They had seen it coming for some time, of course, and so had he. Yet even he had been surprised by the God-forsakenness of it.[38] As for them, they had anticipated events as a wife anticipates the death of a sick husband. She thinks she knows what that bereavement will mean, and she gets herself ready for it, but when it arrives it turns out to be a stranger, and her grief has a terrible novelty. So they had not foreseen the hopelessness, the sharp guilt, the desolation, the emptiness. It was only then, as the city and its crosses were lost to sight behind the ridge, that they realised quite how much hope they had pinned on him. They had not understood him for the most part, but now they recalled those moments when the light had flickered in their minds and they had seen him, or thought they had seen him, for who he really was. Then hope had leapt inside them, hope not only for themselves, not only for their own people, but (how ridiculous it seemed now) for the whole world, for God and his entire creation.

Those moments had deceived them. There was no point to them. They had been wrong. It was all finished, and there was nothing to do but walk back to Galilee, where it had all begun. What they would do when they got there, they did not ask. One thing at a time. Keep walking. Think of the hardness of the parched earth beneath the soles of the feet. Fix the mind on thirst, on hunger: they were hungry and thirsty enough. Fix it on anything but those three crosses behind them, the other side of the ridge.

Three days out from Jerusalem they came to Galilee, and to the southern shore of its sea. For the last few miles they had had to struggle against a cold wind blowing from the north. Its force had steadily increased as they came nearer to the lake. Bent double, they fought their way to the top of the final hill. At its summit they collapsed on the ground, stopped by the sheer ferocity of the gale, and by their own amazement and terror. The lake was in a fury. This was no ordinary storm. The waves had a viciousness about them, as if they had some monstrous, demonic life of their own, and the wind bore with it the stench of death, the smell of ruthless power, of fear and despair. Even crucifixion had not been like this, or rather it had – but not on this scale, not writ so large. They fell to the ground and wrapped their cloaks about their heads.

They lay there for hours, like corpses strewn among the rocks, when a high-pitched sound, quite at odds with the chaos of the surrounding noise, made them raise their heads. It was the crying of a bird. In the howl of the wind and the crashing of the waves it came to them, and there it was, circling above the lake, its white wings flashing as it turned. It knew the wind well, and was master of it, even of that unnatural storm. It soared and dipped and pivoted, and its cry was like the distant laughter of a child. Yet still the storm raged. The bird rose higher and higher, until to their gaze it seemed like a bright, circling star in the grey sky.

Then, all of a sudden the bird folded its wings and dived. Clean through the storm it fell, while the world held its breath. With a splash, quite inaudible above the wind, it disappeared beneath the waves. At that moment, in the twinkling of an eye, the storm died and the waves crumpled and collapsed into calm. Those on the shore scarcely noticed. Their eyes were fixed on the small point where the bird had disappeared. They waited for it to emerge.

An age passed. Then one of the women saw it first, some way from the place where it had entered the water, floating easily, rocked by the swell. As they straightened up, their eyes on the bird, they sensed for the first time the death of the storm, and felt the calm overtake them.

The silence was broken by a cry from the bird, as it rose lightly from the water. It flew towards them, calling continually, and rose in smooth circles above their heads. In the darkness of the storm it had seemed pure white. Now, in the sun, the tips of its wings were tinged with red, as if stained with blood. As it flew higher only the whiteness remained, until, very high now, that too became one with the dazzle of the sun.

It was finished.

❧22 The Sunflower

All about was desolation. The stale, stinking canal, the old Victorian tenements, the streets with the rubbish of last month still piled in the gutters, the lamp-posts broken. Some of the flats were boarded up, others had their windows broken, all, or nearly all, looked sad, tired, and as if they should have been pulled down years ago. Stone sinks on the stairs, privies in the back yards, two or three rooms for a family of five or six. There are many places like it, and worse.

At first glance, or even second or third glance, there was nothing of beauty to be seen anywhere. There was no grass, and no trees grew there. Some of the children had never seen trees. Yet, if you looked hard, you might catch sight of a geranium in a high-perched window-box, while on the end of one terrace someone had painted a large mural of mountains and fields and birds flying in a blue sky – but the 'NF Rules OK' scrawled across it did not fit in with the design.

At the end of Jubilee Street the desolation was complete. For thirty years the bomb site had been there, ever since a German incendiary had fallen on old Mabel and Arthur, asleep in their bed in the front room downstairs. No one had ever been able to persuade them to go down to the shelter in the air raids. No one had ever found their bodies. For thirty years the bomb site had been their only memorial, empty, broken, bearing no inscription. No one had ever put any flowers there. It was covered instead with broken pieces of masonry and the inevitable litter. It defeated even the most vigorous and persistent weeds.

Nothing grew there, until one autumn a seed took root. The following spring nobody noticed the plant for several weeks, but in the end you cannot miss a sunflower. There it stood, five or six feet tall, with its heavy, golden head. When the sun was out, its yellow was so intense that people would shield their eyes against it, but on dull days, and most days were overcast in Jubilee Street, it shone almost as powerfully as if a strange light of its own burned within its petals.

It caused quite a stir. Most of the local people had never seen a sunflower and, if they had, they had not seen one quite like that. Nothing had grown on their bomb site before. They would gather round in small groups, looking at it, wondering what to do with it. There were a few who were cheered by its beauty. Of those, some were changed by it. That sunflower lifted them out of the drabness of their world, and their own drabness fell off them. You could tell them by the way they walked. They no longer had that tired, dejected stoop, so characteristic of the inhabitants of those streets. Most people, however, were merely bewildered. They did not know what to make of the flower. It was so out of place. It did not fit, and you could not write 'NF Rules OK' all over it to make it fit.

So they just left it alone, and thought they would get used to it. But they did not. It was so conspicuous with that strange light it had, and its piercing yellow. It showed up the drabness, the desolation, all around for what it was: empty, ugly, dead. That was why after a time most of the people grew to be so bitter about it. It had led a few out of the wilderness, but the rest it had left there, recognising for the first time what sort of place they lived in. They could not see the path leading out of their desert, and so they remained there trapped, and for the first time *feeling* trapped. It became intolerable. You must not blame them.

You or I would have done the same, feeling as they did. One evening they went in a great crowd to the bomb site, and they trampled on that sunflower, and danced on it, and beat the fibres of its leaves and stem into the ground, and crushed its petals till they were but a stain which the dust soon covered. Then they went away in silence, their job done.

Yet they destroyed that strange plant in high summer, when its flower was full of ripe seed. In their dance of death they scattered that seed over the entire bomb site, and buried some of it in the ground. So it was that next spring the bomb site at the end of Jubilee Street was covered with sunflowers.

There were flowers on Mabel's and Arthur's grave at last.

He watched from behind some large, black rocks as the man from Nazareth came once more to his kingdom. He let him pass by, then slid out from his hiding place and called after him. 'Here I am, Jesus, behind you!' His voice moved over the face of the wilderness, and called forth its desolation. 'Have you had second thoughts, that you come here again? Are you prepared now to accept my propositions, agree to our little plan?'

He circled slowly round Jesus, looking as if he might pounce at any moment. 'We could be a great team, you and I. Look at all you have achieved! And in such a short space of time, too! Few could have become such a conspicuous failure in such a short time as you have done! Yet I have been impressed by you. You have great potential, Jesus. If only you had followed my advice in the first place, things would not have come to this. But it is not too late.'

His circling began to get faster. 'We could try again, try this time to impress the right people, try this time to work some miracles out in the open, in the market place, where people will notice. You have been working in alleyways, in dark corners. You have taken the blind and the lame off the stage, away from the bright lights, and healed them in the wings. That won't do. Razzmatazz! Razzmatazz! That's what we need!'

By now he was dancing a weird, frenetic jig. 'Let me be your director, and I will make you a star, Jesus! They might even get to calling you "Son of God"! You see, it's not *what* you do that's wrong, it's the way that you do it.'

Suddenly he slowed down, and resumed his measured, sinister prowl. 'I have heard that you walked on the water, and calmed a storm.[40] But I did not see it. I was there. I always am, aren't I, Jesus? But I did not see anything. I have many friends living round the Sea of Galilee, but they saw nothing, heard nothing. Some of them were out in boats at the time, but they did not catch your footfall on the waves, nor did the storm cease for them. Two of them were drowned. I knew them well. Why did you not save *them*, Jesus? Were they the wrong side of the lake? You have to be the right side of the lake to get saved, Jesus, is that it? To the devil with the rest, is that it?' He laughed.

'Now, if you and I were in partnership, we could save everybody, no questions asked. "Salvation for all!" That could be our motto, and people could have it whether they wanted it or not. After all, salvation is salvation, never mind how you come by it.'

At last he stopped, and stood waiting for an answer.

'You and your friends are so hard of hearing,' said Jesus, 'so blind to what is around you, so dead to all feeling! Did you sense nothing at all, as you lay there in the dark turbulence of those waters? Did you not feel anything as I stepped upon your back, as I touched your wild chaos with my finger, and raised my hand to give you my blessing? I suppose you were expecting me to walk all over you with hobnailed boots. But that is not my way, Satan. I have a light touch. I do things on the quiet. You do not know the meaning of gentleness. Yet I had hoped you would feel one footstep, and begin to feel my calm. I had wanted your friends to see just a little beneath the surface, to sense my creation beneath your destruction. One day they will find it. You do not believe me, Satan, but my gentleness is stronger than your violence, my humility more enduring than your arrogance, and my laughter and my love lie too deep for your bitterness and cynicism.'

'Come, then!' said Satan savagely, and he stepped forward, as if to take hold of Jesus. 'Come, let me take you to the top of a high mountain, and show you the kingdoms of the world and the glory of them!'[41]

They turned and went up together, till they reached the very summit and the world lay at their feet.

'Look!' shouted Satan against the howl of the wind. 'Look, there they are! The petty kingdoms of this paltry world! You could have had them for your own, if only you had been willing to co-operate. But see, they are mine! Look at them tearing each other apart, dismembering the world! You have heard it said:

"Thou hast made him little less than God,
and dost crown him with glory and honour."[42]

But what I say to you is this:

"I have made him little higher than the demons,
and girded him with lust and greed!"

I have made these precious human beings of yours the most aggressive and destructive of all your creatures. The earthworm and the orchid may not yet be mine, nor the antelope and the wren, but humanity at least is mine! You have lost them, Jesus! You have lost, lost, Jesus!' The hideous dance began again, but Jesus did not wait this time for it to cease.

'You see only the dark,' Jesus cried. 'You do not see in the dark, you see only the darkness itself, and you teach others to do the same.'

'And you see only the sunset, the daffodil, and the butterfly!' shouted Satan as he spat on the rocks.

'If I see only them, then I see more than you do, Satan. But, no. I see the dark, also.'

'But you do not *know* the dark as I know it. You do not see it for what it is.'

Jesus pointed to scars on his hands and feet. 'Do you not recognise them, Satan? You put them there yourself. Oh, I know your darkness. I have been there, but you were so blind, you did not notice me. Now I have come out of the dark, Satan, into the light, the light that I created, the light that is myself. You had no hold over me in the beginning, and you have none now. I am risen from the dead, Satan, and everywhere there is resurrection! Your days are numbered, and one day this wilderness of yours will become again the garden of God.'

Satan no longer heard him because of the howl of the wind, and he did not see through the mist clinging to his mountain top, as Jesus walked down the mountain side towards those petty kingdoms of this paltry world. He was left a solitary figure on the summit, mesmerised by his own deadly dance, leaping and jerking in unending circles round nothing but himself.

✸ 24 The Homecoming

From the beginning of time this had been a desert place. Nothing had ever grown here, nothing could ever survive here as far as anyone could imagine. The vast areas of sand and rock surrounding it had once, many centuries before, been covered with forest, or, crisscrossed by irrigation channels, had supported thousands of cattle, sheep and goats, and field upon field of grain. But not this place. This was true wilderness: sterile, barren, a cruel, hard place, a place of paralysed chaos, where no order seemed able to emerge. A place of no hope. Any track leading towards it veered away, or stopped at its edge. Even the insane went no farther.

Yet once, yet twice, he went there, and not just to its borders, but to the dead heart of it.

The first time he slipped in uncertainly, merging in his frailty with the dust and the rock.[43] There was no fuss, no noise, nothing to see, but in that wilderness his mercy, his humility and his love were put on the rack, tried by all that was merciless and life-defeating. The forces of darkness gathered their strength to twist and stretch, to pull and tear him. They did not prevail. He slipped out again, without fuss, without noise, without spectacle, and returned to human company, his mercy, humility and love now as strong as steel.

Once more he went there, this time not uncertainly. He came as a conqueror, as one who had already won the victory, and the forces of darkness retreated, cowered among the rocks, dared not cross his path. He strode through the dust and across the bare rock, casting no shadow as he went, leaving flowers in his footsteps. Behind him came the creatures of the desert. They arrived in their thousands, running, crawling, sliding in his wake. The insects came too, and the birds.

The sky above the place had once been as barren as the ground, but now insects in their millions danced their eternal dance of life in humming, iridescent clouds, the butterflies fluttered about him, enlivening the air with the bright gaiety of their wings, while up there, high up there in the sudden bright blue, the eagles and the kites wove a crown for him with the circling patterns of their great wings.

Before this multitude, this noisy celebration, the forces of darkness fled, fled towards a low depression in the dead centre of the place. There he came. As he reached the edge of the hollow, the animals behind him slipped into the shadows of the rocks, the insects ceased their humming and settled on the ground, and the birds hung motionless in the sky.

They waited. He did not. He went on without pause, down towards the middle of the depression. There, in the centre, was a large, broken rock, with a strange horn jutting out from its side, tapering to its point some seven feet from the ground. From that arm of rock hung a rope, and from the rope hung a man. Though a sudden storm howled and shrieked, and snatched repeatedly at the body, causing it to swing wildly to and fro, he, the conqueror, marched up to the rock, took the man down, untied the rope from his neck, and laid him on his shoulder.

At that moment the wind died. The animals, the insects and the flowers invaded the hollow, and the eagles and kites and falcons flew above it – tumbling, twisting, swooping in their ecstasy.

They stayed in that place and made their homes there, the animals and the birds, the insects and the flowers, though he left them, bearing the body of the man on his shoulder.

In heaven, joy knew no bounds. They had waited a long time for this. They had missed him. They had needed his company. But now he had come home, riding on the shoulders of the one he had once betrayed. They killed a fatted calf for him, dressed him up like a king, put a ring on his finger and sandals on his feet,[44] and wept and cheered as once again the betrayer and the betrayed embraced.

God's Forgiveness[45]

There was once a man who had two sons. But I am only going to tell you about one of them. Let the other, the elder son, be another story.

It happened one day that the younger son reached the magical age of eighteen. He had come of age; he was officially mature. So he went to his father, and he did what he thought all people did when they became mature: he asked for some money, lots of it.

'I want to go my own way now, Dad, do my own thing', he said. 'In fact, now I'm eighteen, Dad,' he said, 'I *demand* I go my own way. I have a right to my freedom, and if I don't get what is my right, then I shall take it. You look as though you've got a good few years in you yet, Dad, and I can't wait for the money you'll leave me when you die. So if you want to avoid any unpleasantness, Dad, just hand it over now, there's a good Dad.'

Dad did as he was told.

So the son went out and spent some of the money on a nice little Suzuki 250 cc and, his pockets bulging with the rest, he roared off into the sunset. His father watched him go, and was still watching even after his son had disappeared out of sight over the brow of the hill.

Now I know what you're thinking. You're thinking that the son went off to the city and helped himself straight away to a huge helping of riotous living, and came back for seconds. Well, you're wrong. He did go to the city, but for a time he lived fairly quietly. He looked after Number 1, all right. He had a good time, a bit of self-indulgence here, and a bit of self-indulgence there, and not much indulgence of anybody else, but he didn't go mad, if you know what I mean. Not for a bit, anyway.

Not till he met Her. Isn't there supposed to be something soft about women? Not this one. She was so hard, you could have cut diamonds with her! Yet our hero worshipped her. He had his riotous living then, all right, and in no time at all his money was gone, and his motorbike was gone (he sold it to buy drugs for his goddess), and in no time at all she was gone. That's when living stopped being quite so riotous. In fact, living became existing, became deadly. He ended up – I can hardly bring myself to tell you, for the tears welling up in my eyes and the lump coming to my throat – he ended up working for British Rail . . . as a porter . . . at Clapham Junction . . . platform 53 (freight trains only) . . . sleeping in the waiting room by night, dining in the canteen by day . . . every day eating three-month-old pork pies and drinking the last of yesterday's brew from the tea-urn.

It took him two weeks, three days, four hours, nine minutes and forty-six seconds to come to his senses. It happened during lunch. He found a cockroach in his tea. That was his moment of truth. He picked up his cup of tea and what was left of his pork pie, went to the station manager's office, knocked, entered, walked over to the station manager, took off the station manager's hat, turned it upside down, put his pork pie inside it, and his tea, placed the hat back on the station manager's head, carefully, pushed it down hard, and left for home.

His father was still watching for him, still looking at the point where the road disappeared over the hill. Four days after leaving Clapham Junction he arrived, on foot. You will remember he no longer had a motorbike, and the buses were on strike. His father saw him as he appeared slowly over the brow of the hill, and he ran, despite the stiffness of his legs — well, your legs would have been stiff if you had stood watching for as long as he had — he ran to meet him. And as he approached him, the father cried out, 'My son, my son! You're home!' and went to fling his arms round him. But the son walked up to him, dealt him a vicious blow to the jaw and kicked him into the ditch, and marched on to help himself to the rest of his father's estate.

He did not look back. Had he done so, he would have seen his father crawl out of the ditch, and he would have seen too the empty embrace and the lips moving in silent words of blessing.

❧26 Dead Centre

It stood at the end of the main street, the world's first spherical office block. It had taken nine years to build, and had presented the architects, the engineers and the builders with more problems than three Sydney Opera Houses. It lay within a mesh of narrow steel girders, which bore some resemblance to the outer structure of a gasometer.

Within its cradle the globe slowly revolved. It did not turn all the time. Between 5.30 each evening and 9.00 each morning it stood silent and motionless. Nine o'clock sharp was when the master of the enterprise sat down at his desk of a morning and pressed the switch to his right that started the building turning. Half-past five each evening was when he flicked up the switch, picked up his hat and coat, and made for the door of his lift. None of the thousands who worked around him in the building could leave till he had flicked the switch and departed. All of them had to make quite sure they were inside and at their desks before the switch was pressed in the morning.

The private office of the master was itself a near sphere and lay at the dead centre of the building. It was the only room that did not turn. All revolved around it. It was ringed by twelve wedge-shaped offices, one for each of the master's chief executives. No door led from this circle of offices into the central sphere, nor did any windows look into it. The master conducted his business with those around him entirely by means of a series of electronic devices. None of his employees even knew what he looked like. In the centre of his office was a shaft containing the lift that brought him up each morning from his own personal car park, buried deep underground.

At first, admittedly, he had not been the only one to use that lift. Important visitors from other companies had come to do business with him, to be won over by his devastating charm, and then to be destroyed by his cleverness. Some of them, driven by his ploys into bankruptcy, or drowning in his corruption, lost hope and committed suicide. Others passed the word around before it was too late. Eventually no one dared to use the lift to his office, and from then on he sat at his desk in a perpetual solitary state, with only the company of his desk and his gadgetry.

The time came when that solitariness became absolute. The thousands who worked around him, turning slowly on his axis, got to the point when they could bear it no longer. One by one, ten by ten, and fifty by fifty, they left, until the day came when no one turned up for work save the master himself. He left his car in his car park, ascended by the central lift, as he always did, entered his office at 8.59 as usual, hung up his coat, sat down at his desk, and pressed the small switch to his right.

The reassuring hum of the building's turning began. For half an hour the sphere turned around him, empty, silent, and for half an hour he tried in vain to get some response from his communication systems. At the end of it he knew he was alone. He remained sitting quietly at his desk, staring with blank eyes at the far wall of his office. He sat like that for several hours, lashed by the mounting waves of his loneliness. Finally he made up his mind. He opened the second drawer down on the left, took out a penknife, opened the sharpest blade and, without bothering to leave a note (for who would read it?), cut his wrists.

He had forgotten to flick up the switch.

So it was that he was brought, somewhat prematurely, to the City of God. He found himself, to his surprise, inside another spinning sphere. But this one needed no cage of girders to support it. Driven by God's merriment, it had no blank walls either, no private office, no solitariness. At the heart of it, not outside the walls this time, but at its still centre, stood a cross. Upon that cross he, the master of his deadly little world, was hung. His small-mindedness was hung upon the generosity of God, his ruthlessness stretched upon God's most uncomfortable humility. There in agony they died and, seeing them die, the Master of the city came and took him down, and laid him gently in the garden tomb of his love, and raised him up upon the third day.

Far below, the office building at the end of the main street stopped turning.

❦ 27 The Ladder

I stuck out my tongue, the man at the gate took the coin, the turnstile clicked seven times, and I was through, on the far side of the barrier.

It was like Brighton Pier in the old days, when it was at its prime, except that I could no longer hear the sea. It had sounded continuously in my ears the other side of the turnstile. Now there was only a strange silence. But I had no time to work things out. I found myself in a small round room, lined entirely with mirrors. I was on my own. I could not escape from myself. Wherever I looked, there I was, looking back at myself. I tried to close my eyes, but my eyelids would not obey me. The mirrors were full of curious distortions, and there were areas that seemed lightly frosted where my image was obscure. Yet gradually those patches cleared, the distortions disappeared, and for the first time I saw myself as I was.

There were moments then when I tried desperately to shut my eyes, I can tell you, but still my eyelids refused to let in the merciful dark. Instead the mirrors became clearer and clearer, and it was as if I was turned inside out and was looking at what lay within myself. I do not mean that I got an all-round picture of my pulsating brain, or an inside view of my alimentary canal. I mean that I could not pretend any more, I could not hide any more from who I was. It was all unnerving. Sometimes it made me weep, though the tears were not always ones of shame or sorrow. I had not recognised much of the goodness in me either.

The mirrors then began to cloud over, and when they cleared for a second time I saw not myself, but myself as I had imagined myself to be. I saw only the surface, the surface I had believed was me, the surface I had tried to make others believe was me. I pointed at myself in the mirrors and burst out laughing.

With the force of my laughter the glass shattered and dissolved, and I found myself beyond the little room, standing on a rung of a wide ladder that seemed to stretch from earth to heaven. Now I was no longer alone. All humankind was on this ladder, all, that is, as had passed through the barrier. Some were below me, some above, some far, far ahead. I knew them all. I recognised every one. All of us had been turned inside out. There was no hiding anything from anyone. We could not keep our identity tags underneath our vests. We had no vests, you see.

Most of this vast multitude were climbing slowly upwards, but some were clinging to the ladder, refusing to go any higher, frightened to take another step, while others had turned and were coming down. I stood amazed. Then a great fear came over me, and locked my fingers to the rung above my head. The ladder seemed to go upwards for ever. There was no end to it, though it disappeared into faint light far above and, still stretching on, was gone. I shut my eyes to the light, and pressed myself to the ladder.

Someone touched my shoulder, and hands slowly uncurled my fingers and loosened my grip. He was not like the rest, for his identity was hidden from me. Gently he took my arm, and we began the ascent.

I cannot tell you all there is to tell about the climb. Suffice it to say the rungs passed more easily the higher I got. It was as if I was leaving behind the forces of gravity, losing all that weighed me down. Suffice it to say that the light became brighter and grew to a glare that pierced me almost beyond endurance. The stranger beside me strengthened his grip on my arm, shielded my eyes with his other hand, and so we went on into the light beyond the glare. Have you ever had the experience of seeing the truth about something with absolute clarity? There, in the light beyond the glare, was the truth about all things. Have you been overwhelmed by great beauty or goodness? I tell you, all beauty, all goodness, were there. Have you ever had the sense of being deeply loved? Absolute love was there.

I knew, because I was in the midst of truth, the identity of the stranger who had unlocked my fingers and brought me there. He was beside me no longer, but was all about me. And as I looked I saw his light on all the people, the vast multitude of people at this stage on the ladder. The light shone from their faces, as I sensed it must shine from mine.

The ladder leads ever onwards, ever upwards, further into the heart of the light. There is no end to it. How can there be, since there is no end to God?

28 Speaking of God

NARRATOR: To speak of God is to do the unspeakable, to touch the holy that cannot be touched, to unveil what for eternity must remain a mystery. Yet men and women will have their say. Discontent with mere bread and wine, so heavy with the holy, not satisfied with words from a mountain top written with the finger of God, bored by the silence of the wilderness, men and women will have their say.

ADAM: I, Adam, speak of the loneliness of God.

EVE: We speak, you and I, of the loneliness of God. We can still see it, you know. If you look there from these acres of thorns and thistles, if you look into the sun, you can see it quite clearly. Do you see? There, where the sun is brightest and best, a splash of green on the canvas of the desert, green of palm, cypress and olive, green of oak and Scots pine, the startling green of beech in the spring.

ADAM: A place not just for the desert man newly formed from the dust . . .

EVE: Or the woman new sprung from the rib . . .

BOTH: But for all humankind, a place for all creation.

ADAM: There the wolf lies down with the lamb, and the leopard with the kid. There Cain might have played over the hole of the asp, and Abel put his hand on the adder's den.[46] There we might still have walked with God in the cool of the day, you and I.[47] As it is, he has his garden to himself now, and walks there by himself.

BOTH: We speak of the loneliness of God.

CAIN: I speak of the homelessness of God. I cannot see Eden. For me it is ever beyond the ridge, out of my knowing, always, always to the west. I bear on my forehead the mark of God, like those who have been tossed by the Spirit of God on the waters of baptism.[48] I do not belong here. I have no belonging anywhere, no place to call my own. They do not know me, or they know me only too well. I am always turning, returning, restless, bearing on my forehead the mark of God. I keep company with the scapegoat.

And yet, do you know what I have heard from the creatures of the wilderness? He has been here, so they tell me, and still has nowhere where he may lay his head.[49] For all I know he is hereabouts even now, as restless as I am. I, Cain, can begin to speak of the homelessness of God.

ABRAHAM: I speak to you of the strangeness of God.

I, Abraham, who have stretched a knife over my son, my only son, whom I love and loved then, Isaac,[50] I who have brought all God's hope, all God's generosity, all God's saying 'It is good, it is good, it is very good'[51] to within a hair's breadth of catastrophe, I can speak to you of the strangeness of God. And all I can say to you is this: I do not understand, yet in the end is such relief and delight and strong embrace and the sweet smell of roast ram and dancing down a mountain to the tune of 'The Lord provides!', a bells-on-the-ankles-knees-up-Mother-Brown of a tune! Do you know it?

Oh yes, I can speak of the strangeness of God!

JACOB: Then I can speak of the playfulness of God.

JONAH: So can I! When you have seen the inside of the stomach of death and a fish, you have plenty to say about the playfulness of God![52]

JACOB: But I had him! I *had* him! I had *Him*![53] I have the name to prove it: 'Israel', which means, Jonah, 'one who has striven with God, and *has prevailed*'![54] That was my game, Jonah! Yours was hopscotch by comparison!

JONAH: Indeed it was! Playing hopscotch with God in the middle of Berlin, in the corridors of Gestapo headquarters![55] I have seen as much of the playfulness of God as you, Jacob Israel.

JACOB: I had him pinned there, betrayed, scourged, mocked, nailed there! He was in my power! And still I escaped with my life, and now all the talk is of resurrection. There's a game for you!

JONAH: The trouble is, he refuses to play by our rules. And what is the result? Repentance!

JACOB: And grace upon grace.

JONAH: And our small-mindedness.

JACOB: Joy at last.

JONAH: And our bewilderment.

BOTH: Yes, though the falcons tell it best, where they twist and spin and tumble fall where the cliff goes sharp to the sea, though they tell it best, we too can speak of the playfulness of God.

MOSES: And I can speak of the fathoms of his mystery.

SOLOMON: And I, the great Solomon, who have seven hundred wives, princesses all of them, and three hundred concubines, do not have the time to speak to you about anything.[56]

MOSES: I was the last, you will remember, to see him face to face.[57] It began noisily, but in the end it was a quiet transfiguration, away from the crowd. It reminded me of a fire in a desert bush, God's light among the thorns.[58] I have seen that somewhere else. I, Moses, speak of the dark fathoms of his mystery.

JOB: And I, Job, crushed, as I thought, by his foot, stamped on, beaten to a pulp by his fists, once yelping my anger, storming his dark heaven with my blasphemies,[59] I now can only speak of her delight in things for which I have little or no concern, and tell you of her gentle mothering.[60] She leads the darkness by the hand (did you know that?), gives birth to the ice, wraps the chaos of the ocean in its cot blanket and sings it a lullaby, asking the sons of God to stop shouting for joy for a while, plays midwife to the mountain goat.[61] Her love goes far away, far beyond mine. My world is so small, so tent-sized, compared with hers. I lay my hand on my mouth. I have spoken once, and I will not answer; twice, but I will proceed no further.

ALL, EXCEPT JOB: You have spoken what is right, Job. We also lay our hands on our mouths. We will proceed no further.

ALL: To speak of God is to do the unspeakable, to touch the holy that cannot be touched, to unveil what for eternity must remain a mystery. We will proceed no further.

 Notes

1 The Song of Songs 2.10–12, adapted.
2 cf Genesis 9.20–27.
3 cf Genesis 17.17.
4 cf Exodus 32.1–6.
5 Psalm 88.3–4,6–7, adapted.
6 cf Mark 5.1–20 and parallels.
7 cf Exodus 33.18–23.
8 cf Genesis 3.10.
9 cf Genesis 2.10–14.
10 'The Lost Son' has its beginnings in the Cain and Abel story (Genesis 4.1–17), and finds its ending in the crucifixion of Jesus, and in particular in the story of the penitent thief in Luke's account (Luke 23.39–43).
11 cf Genesis 4.17.
12 cf Genesis 1.2.
13 cf Exodus 33.18–23.
14 'The Tower' is loosely based on the Tower of Babel story in Genesis 11.1–9, and in some respects turns that story on its head.
15 cf Job 38.7.
16 A meditation on the Abraham and Isaac story in Genesis 22.1–19.
17 cf Genesis 12.10–20 and 20.1–18 (notice the 'at every place' of 20.13).
18 One of Stanley Spencer's paintings in his 'Christ in the Wilderness' series is entitled 'The Scorpion', and shows Christ holding a scorpion in his hands.
19 cf Genesis 3.8.
20 Song of Songs 4.9–11, in Marcia Falk's translation in *Love Lyrics from the Bible*, Almond Press, 1982.
21 The image of God in the wilderness with the scapegoat was suggested to me by Robert Graves' poem 'In the Wilderness'.
22 cf 1 Kings 19.9,13.
23 See my interpretation of 1 Kings 19.1–18 in *Lo and Behold! The power of Old Testament storytelling*, pp 118–124.
24 Song of Songs 8.6–7a, again Marcia Falk's translation.
25 An oblique reference to Jesus' entry into Jerusalem, which was, of course, the prelude to his arrest, trials and crucifixion.
26 Clearly 'God's Passion' draws upon the Garden of Eden story in Genesis 2–3 and the book of Jonah. A less obvious, though equally important source, is the image of God's 'marriage' to Israel found in Hosea 1–3, Isaiah 54.4–8, and Jeremiah 2.2.
27 cf Jonah 1.2.
28 In Hosea 14.4–7 the prophet pictures God singing a love song (the language is reminiscent of the Song of Songs) to a 'male' Israel. By implication God plays the part there of a woman in love.

29 'God's Mountain' combines elements of the account in Exodus 19 of God's appearance at Sinai with features of Jesus' birth and infancy narratives in Matthew and Luke. In the final section of the story there is a thinly veiled reference to 1 Kings 19.11–13.

30 cf Exodus 33.11.

31 cf Isaiah 40.3–5.

32 cf Matthew 7.7.

33 See note 23 above.

34 cf John 13.3–5.

35 'The Wine-Maker' is based on John 2.1–11, the story of the miracle of the wedding at Cana.

36 cf Exodus 6.6 and 12.8.

37 'The Grass-Eater' draws not only on material from the Gospels, but on the children's book *Tiger Flower* by Robert Vavra and Fleur Cowles, Collins, 1968.

38 cf Mark 15.34.

39 cf Matthew 4.1–11 and its parallel in Luke 4.1–13.

40 cf Mark 4.35–41 and 6.45–52 and parallels.

41 cf Matthew 4.8 and Luke 4.5–6.

42 Psalm 8.5.

43 cf Matthew 4.1–11; Luke 4.1–13.

44 cf Luke 15.22–23.

45 A variation on the first part of the Parable of the Prodigal Son, Luke 15.11–24.

46 cf Isaiah 11.6,8.

47 cf Genesis 3.8.

48 cf Genesis 4.15.

49 cf Matthew 8.20.

50 cf Genesis 22.1–19.

51 cf Genesis 1.4,10,12,18.

52 cf Jonah 1.17–2.10.

53 cf Genesis 32.22–32.

54 cf Genesis 32.28.

55 Jonah 3. See my reading of the Jonah story in *Lo and Behold!*, ch 7, 'God's Fool II: This time in Berlin'.

56 cf 1 Kings 11.3.

57 cf Exodus 33.11.

58 cf Exodus 3.2 and the crown of thorns worn by Jesus at the crucifixion in all the account except Luke's.

59 cf Job, especially chs 9–10,12, 16–17, 19.

60 The first of God's two great speeches towards the end of the book of Job (chs 38–39) contains or suggests an unusual number of feminine images of God.

61 For the images in this sentence cf. Job 38.19–20, 29, 8–9, 7; 39.1–4.

Also by Trevor Dennis:

Lo and Behold!
The Power of Old Testament Storytelling

'*Lo and Behold!* is a book which illustrates the power of Old Testament stories by a sensitive and intelligent re-telling of some of its most significant narratives. Trevor Dennis writes for all who find the Old Testament a struggle. He has a marvellous feel for the Hebrew text and manages to convey its directness and subtlety in vivid, conversational English.'   *Church Times*

'A vastly entertaining and illuminating book . . . people won't be able to say the Old Testament is dull after reading this.'   *Methodist Recorder*

'A thoroughly enjoyable study . . . it recovers for us the delightful freshness, literary genius, humour and audacity of the original.'   *Catholic Herald*

'Exhilarating reading . . . highly recommended.' *Alpha*

'Strongly recommended for study groups, for those unfamiliar with the Old Testament or jaded by other methods of study.'   *Theological Book Review*

'A brilliant and exciting excursion through Genesis to Kings . . . If you have ever wished you could make more sense of the God of the Old Testament, then get this most readable of books and re-read the stories with it.'   *Reform*

Lo and Behold! is published by SPCK, priced £9.99

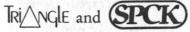 and **SPCK**
Books
can be obtained from
all good bookshops.
In case of difficulty,
or for a complete list of our books,
contact:
SPCK Mail Order
36 Steep Hill
Lincoln
LN2 1LU
(tel: 01522 527 486)